To
Janet,
Welcome Hor!
Jan Noble

# Home With God

## The Restoration of Your Spiritual Self

JAN NOBLE

**BALBOA.**
PRESS

A DIVISION OF HAY HOUSE

*Balboa Press books may be ordered through booksellers or by contacting:*

*Balboa Press*
*A Division of Hay House*
*1663 Liberty Drive*
*Bloomington, IN 47403*
*www.balboapress.com*
*1-(877) 407-4847*

*ISBN: 978-1-4525-4805-0 (sc)*
*ISBN: 978-1-4525-4806-7 (e)*

*Library of Congress Control Number: 2012903942*

*Printed in the United States of America*

*Balboa Press rev. date: 03/16/2012*

To my children, Laura, Michael and Steven,
and my sister, Darleen, and to Doris Smith,
for remembering the little girl next door.

# ACKNOWLEDGEMENTS

With deep gratitude, I would like to thank the following people (angels) for their love, support, encouragement, patience and assistance: My sister, Darleen Clark, who has served as my spiritual guidepost for decades; my children, Laura Nelson, Michael Fernandez and Steven Fernandez, for tolerating my early years of haphazard mothering and for teaching me the true meaning of unconditional love; my best friend, Verneen Caporgno, for letting me test my theories on her for years, even when she was convinced I was entertaining lunacy; my dear friends and HLI instructors—Sandi Wolfe, Phyliss Hill, Sandy Worthington, Patti Vargas, Mandy Sahota, Debbie Libhart, Debbi Luttrell, Gale Mellow, Carolyn Davis, June Milich, Charlie Sanders (webmaster), Bret Lampman (editing), John Welsh, Jennifer Brewster (office assistant), Pamela Munoz, Shirley Rudel, Michaelle Sheridan, Sam Shamoon, Emily Issac, Sarah Branshaw, Becky Chavez, Sandy Sullivan, Agustin Aragon and Michael Freemire. In addition, I would like to thank my many HLI students, who for fifteen years have provided proof that spirit exists in all humans through their demonstrations of empowerment and dedication. Lastly, I want to thank Mom. She knows why.

# INTRODUCTION

I've always envisioned the "battle of good and evil" as being between a menacing dungeon dragon (our collective ego) and a magnificent white stallion (our collective spirit) fighting for the soul of humanity and the restoration of its true spiritual self. I believe that in our deepest heart, every human on earth has a profound longing for the side of the stallion (spirit) to win the battle of good and evil because, on an almost forgotten level of awareness, each of us occasionally is gifted with a brief visit *Home with God* and a glimpse of remembrance that we are in reality the child of God, lost in the trappings of a dream of our own making. The evil dungeon dragon (ego,) of course, has provided those trappings and squelched much of the memory of being *Home with God* with his fierce, loud boastful bellows of self-aggrandizement and egoistic power. But our ego's only real tool for battle is fear, for his body is made of *nothing!* There is no substance. He is just an illusion of our collective fascination-controlled mind, which loves to excite itself with fear! The moment we choose to end our fascination with *evil* we will turn the word (and the world) back around to its rightful position and begin to truly *live*. This is exactly what I see happening in our world today—the relinquishment of fear and the reversal of ego. The willingness to look through the lens of *Spirit,* which reveals the transparency of ego and the world of illusion, is allowing us to restore our memory of ourselves to our true state of being—*as Spirit embodied*—and to begin the journey *Home with God* . . .

# The Trek

This one was the longest, the most arduous of all
And the loneliest
The Trek
We embarked with visions of conquest, as befits our nature
And tossed all trepidation to the wind
With each other, nothing could be unsurpassable
No peaking cliffs, nor vast expanses
Could distance us from one another or our vision

The first to leave were the most ready
Prepared with sojourns far and wide
Rested and fed and nurtured
Who would have ever thought they would become the need-full
The widest-eyed, lost in a thicket of camouflaged trails

The absence of the warriors sent a piercing alarm
The tone of which has not before resounded with such force
You and I scrambled, vaulting over each other
Rushing to the dance with a long-stemmed rose between our teeth
Sliding down a stairway made of stars

Clearly, we could see our targets for a day or two
Just long enough to slap them on their back
They peered at us as if we were strangers
Perhaps the secret enemy they had been warned to avoid
No amount of convincing could wrangle them away from
forgetfulness
The quicksand had been too deep

Pretty soon, the reunion soured
And we all forgot our pledge
To bring the memory of each other into focus
For the only miscalculation,
The main roadblock to remembering
Was a malfunctioning lens on the port of true perception
The ocean of seeing, obscured by the slightest distortion

How to call the Homeward Trek with the sightless soldiers
Able only to envision that which supports their dream?
How to nudge them into mindfulness of their prior recollection
The memory of Reality they once beheld themselves?
The shaking of their sleepiness, the rousting from their slumber
Without fear?

A gentle whispering; the everyday reminder
Tiny flashes of light beckoning from the corner of the room
The soft rustling of tree branches on a cloudy day
Birds, singing in the early morning hours outside your window
The sound of water; The voice of stillness
Gazing into His eyes as we look to one another
The willingness to recall
Will finally lead us Home . . .

# THE WARRIORS

On my mother's side, there is Cherokee lineage from her grandmother. On my father's side, there is no knowledge of Native American ancestry. Yet when he passed away at the age of 49, my father was collected by a group of six men who looked, to my young mind, like a small band of *Native American warriors*, solemnly bringing his soul home with them.

I was nine years old. It was midnight. Inexplicably, I found myself standing in the middle of the street in front of my house, watching a group of six warriors carry a stretcher holding a man's body out through the front door of the house and down the walkway to the street. Suddenly, I realized that my mother would be upset if she knew that I was standing in the middle of the street at midnight, since I was supposed to be sound asleep in my bed! I also realized as I contemplated my situation that I was in a much larger body, or at least it felt like a larger body, although it seemed to be made of air. The one thing that I was sure of was that I was awake and conscious. This was not a dream.

I watched, mesmerized, as the six warriors placed the stretcher on the curbside behind a vehicle with open back doors. The stretcher stood about four feet high. The warrior standing at the head was the tallest, over six feet in height. The warrior at the foot was slightly shorter, maybe six feet. The other four warriors, two at each side, were all about the same height, an inch or two shorter. They were wearing some type of leggings that stopped just below the knee and sleeveless vests that were open in the front. I don't remember if they were wearing shoes. Their hair was pulled back in a knot or a pony-tail. On their heads, they wore a slender headband with a feather on the left side. On their cheeks, there seemed to be a horizontal streak of dark paint on each side.

To my amazement, the warriors began a *sacred, solemn ceremony* over the man on the stretcher. At this point, I realized the man must be dead. Though I felt like an intruder at this ceremony, I continued to watch silently as the warrior at the head of the stretcher raised his hand and began to write or draw something with his palm in the air above the man's head, while the warrior at the foot of the stretcher did the same thing over the man's feet. The other four simply remained still with their heads bowed. No words were spoken.

As they finished the ceremony and began to lift the stretcher into the vehicle, I came to the startling and extremely distressful realization that the man on the stretcher was my father! Instantly, I returned to my bed and to deep sleep. The following night, my father passed away in his sleep. To this day, I am convinced those warriors came that night to take my father's soul *home* with them . . .

## The Feather

*The words of Spirit are like a feather*
*Wistful, graceful, light*
*Magnificently arranged*
*With the highest purpose*
*Flowing from the wings of angels*
*As they fall into your heart*

*Words from Spirit*
*Touch the deeper meaning*
*Of our existence*
*Bathing insight with tears*
*As we feel the experience*
*Of listening with our heart*
*How could we have forgotten*
*Our words of feathers, our wings*
*That carry our stories of who we truly are?*

*So caught up, we've been*
*In the doing*
*We need to remind ourselves*
*How to Be*
*So busy making time*
*We lost track of timelessness*
*And the still, small voice*
*That carries on the wind*
*Like the feather*

# THE LOST ROAD

For a long time, it seems as though Americans have been traveling down a "lost road." I say lost because for a very long time it appeared as though we had only been looking behind us and failing to see what may lie ahead. For several decades, it seemed as though we had been living in a state of perceived entitlement, without considering the ramifications of our behavior. Greed and acquisition appeared to be in full ruler-ship of our actions. We seemed to be never satisfied with "enough." Then, almost overnight, we discovered that what goes up must come down. The "Great Recession" was upon us. It was thought that our nation might plunge into chaos, or worse. But, inexplicably, something else began to happen. Instead of going up, crime rates fell to their lowest in decades. Charity began to surface as a new neighborhood hallmark, replacing the old "keeping up with the Jones's" attitude of yesteryear. Community and sharing began to spread throughout our nation, fueled by a new sense of responsibility toward our neighbors. "Me" became "Us." "Peace" became our battle-cry.

In his brilliant book, "Winning the War on War: The Decline of Armed Conflict Worldwide," Professor Emeritus of International Relations at American University, Joshua S. Goldstein illustrates how, over the past decade, humanity's longstanding dream of peace is coming true, as he provides careful counts of battle deaths worldwide in the 21st century, revealing records of levels that are half of those in the 1990s and a third of those during the Cold War.

From all appearances, we seem to be moving in another direction, down a new road—one of peace and purpose instead of battle and gain. This road appears to also be spreading across the globe, traveling far and wide, beckoning to people from all walks of life to step onto its higher path. Somehow, on this long experiential trek of ours, we may have made a right turn. Something almost unseen and unheard has been collecting itself on a side path, nudging us back onto a fork in the road toward a future of higher potential and more purposeful lives. Almost surreptitiously, a field of awareness of another way of perceiving our world and ourselves has made its way into the mainstream consciousness of humanity. It is portrayed in the mass media through best-selling books by brilliant authors of science and physics, as well as metaphysics. It is demonstrated as entertainment in film and television, and rendered widely available to a global humanity through the Internet. It has become the new religion of vast numbers of people unwilling to rely on another's testimony and longing for a personal experience of truth and a greater awareness of reality. It is our collective need to go within our own minds and hearts and find our *true source of Being*—our connection to our Creator and to each other. It is our need to remember that we had forgotten something of *tantamount importance*, and then to remember what it was that we had forgotten.

Somewhere in the eons of development of our physical existence, I believe that a seed was planted in our consciousness that has long been dormant, waiting for a catalyst to enable it to germinate. Perhaps now a child has been born with this catalyst, functioning as an activating code in his or her DNA. Science has been aware since the 1980s that children are being born in ever-increasing numbers with advances in their DNA that provide them with expanded physical and mental abilities. Terms for these children include *Indigo, Crystal* and *Rainbow.* Whatever the label, these children exhibit advanced attributes that demonstrate a possibility that humanity may be witnessing a quantum leap in its biological and spiritual evolution. These advancements, attributed to the inexplicable "switching on" of four previously silent DNA codes, enable the children to demonstrate attributes such as higher intelligence quotients, enhanced immune systems, expanded spiritual awareness, highly developed artistic and/or musical talents, psychic abilities, etc. Many of these children have been introduced through film, television and books. You may, however, need only to look in another room of your home to find one of them. They're running around in every neighborhood on earth, disguised as our kids . . . . *and a child will lead the way . . .*

Although the *Indigo* children are a clear indication that something major is occurring in our experience on earth, there are numerous other events taking place in our world that also bear witness to a quantum leap in consciousness. In his groundbreaking book, *The God Code,* Gregg Braden beautifully illustrates the latest scientific discoveries that document evidence of the very *name* of God as it is encoded in every strand of DNA within every cell of every human body on earth. I believe that within this code lies, in addition to the *Indigo* children's expanded attributes, a second mechanism for activating humanity's dormant catalyst and unlocking the seed of higher consciousness. As we read the very words of the text, we are imbued with a sense of enhanced awareness of our own connection to God and we begin to realize that we have been living in a state of *unawareness,* which realization is, in itself, a mechanism for developing awareness. So our first step toward developing a higher awareness of our connection to Spirit would be to *become aware that we have been disconnected* from Spirit, thus enabling the first step toward *the restoration of our spiritual self.*

The disconnection from Spirit is represented in this work as the metaphor of the fiery dungeon dragon, a construct of our ego, which strives to keep us in the dark and unaware of our true nature. Throughout the ages brilliant scribes, speakers, and authors, hoping to restore our memory of our true spiritual nature, have appeared and endeavored to draw our attention to our unwitting reliance on ego as we move through the paces of our lives. This reliance has gone widely unquestioned among the masses for eons. Now, however, in this age of communication, we are seeking answers to questions that have long been swept under the proverbial rug. Home libraries and bookshelves are filling with material that is providing a cornerstone for the building of a new way of thinking and relating to the world in general. People are beginning to see others as an extension of themselves and as another aspect of their Creator. The term, *"There's only One of us here,"* is beginning to make sense. "E Pluribus, Unum"—"From Many, One"—is on every U.S. coin, yet most of us haven't realized that we have been carrying a profound truth in our pockets all along.

Still another global event is taking place today that many believe is a vital aspect of the restoration of our memory of our higher consciousness. Combined with the advent of the highly evolved *Indigo* children and Greg Braden's discoveries of our DNA's inherent connection to and with our Creator, we are in the midst of a galactic event of indefinable proportions—a positioning of our planet within our galaxy that occurs only once every 13,000 years. On sunrise, December 21$^{st}$ in the year 2012, our earth will be aligned with the precise center of the Milky Way galaxy in a way that will bring a "shift" of unprecedented global consciousness that can dramatically change our thoughts, feelings and emotions about ourselves and each other to a more unified, tolerant, familial view of humankind as a whole. This shift is already in evidence as an increase in vibratory frequency for the people of earth and the planet herself, as revealed by the Schumann Resonant Frequency Scale, which has measured a consistent rise in earth's frequency from 7.8 hertz (earth's constant frequency for eons) to now approaching 13 hertz, the frequency our planet will maintain throughout her next galactic spiral.

As earth's frequency rises, so does that of her inhabitants. Vibratory instruments indicate that an average human's frequency is approximately 55 hertz. This is a seven-fold increase of earth's previously constant frequency of 7.8 hertz. If you use seven as a multiplier for earth's upcoming frequency of 13 hertz, it calculates that humanity will eventually be vibrating at approximately 91 hertz during the period after the "shift." At this new frequency, codes in our DNA that have long been dormant can be switched on. These codes are the same ones, I believe, that science is now seeing in the DNA of the *Indigo* children. From my experience, I believe that our DNA is changing at this very moment. As more children are born with the activated codes, we advance toward a time of "critical mass"—a specific date when a certain percentage of earth's population will be universally affected—and, . . . *in the twinkling of an eye* . . . , the advanced attributes previously seen only in the *Indigo* children will broadcast throughout our collective consciousness, download into our collective field of biology. and become mainstream in humanity. I believe that date is the exact same date that earth enters alignment with the precise center of the galaxy—December 21, 2012.

Few people today are completely unfamiliar with these concepts. A list of references is provided in the closing chapter so that you can study this information more thoroughly from some of its many sources. The real purpose of this book is to reveal to you a series of personal experiences, related to these topics, that have occurred over my lifetime and that have literally molded my spiritual life, dramatically changing the way I relate to my friends and family and establishing a life path that I could not have foreseen from my former way of thinking. Also in this text, I introduce the authors, speakers, books, and films that have been brought to my attention, often through somewhat serendipitous experiences, that have enabled me to find my next step along this journey. At the same time I describe here, to the best of my ability, my personal experiences with *Spirit* as they occurred, in the hopes that you will find a spark of recognition in the words and phrases that will, if you choose, assist you to begin, or to rejuvenate, your own trek along the path of higher consciousness, facilitating the restoration of your spiritual self. All of this is designed to accomplish the sharing of an event that will probably last only a brief second or two in your experience. But that brief instant may offer the profound and undeniable realization that you are, always have been, and always will be . . . *Home with God* . . .

## Just One Moment

*All I'm asking you to do*
*Is to take just one moment*
*One far-reaching moment*
*To give consideration to the idea*
*However foreign*
*That You and I are One*
*In all the world and galaxy*
*Even the universe*
*We are the same*
*One being, You and I*

*All I'm asking you to do*
*Is to give pause*
*For a brief moment of time*
*To consider the concept*
*That time is Now*
*And nothing more*
*Past, present and future*
*All rolled into one*
*One time*
*One being, You and I*

*All I'm asking you to do*
*Is to stretch your imagination*
*For a moment*
*To consider the possibility*
*That everything is Here*
*All places, every nook, every cranny*
*Everywhere that ever was*
*Or ever will be*
*Located in One place—Here*
*One time—Now*
*One being—You and I*
*All that is, inside your heart*
*For just One moment . . .*

# THE WILLOW TREE

For the next nine years after my father's death, my adventures into *spirit* consisted mainly of prophetic dreams and periodic episodes of *déjà vu*. My father's death was very hard on my mother and her young family. She suddenly was faced with raising six children on her own. I was second to the oldest. By the late 1960s, I was married and a young mother myself. And then *it* happened again . . .

It was August, 1968. I was eight-and-a-half months pregnant with my son, Michael. My husband and I had decided on the spur of the moment to join his friends and their wives in a brief expedition of frog-gigging on a river that banked a country road near our home. If you've never gigged for frogs, you probably don't know that it must be done on a very dark night, or the frogs may see you lunging toward them with a miniature two-pronged pitchfork and run (or hop) for their lives. My dad had been an outdoorsman and I had been raised, until he died, on mostly wild game, including frog-legs. Once, when I followed him to the river on a camping trip and objected to the ruthless dismemberment of helpless frogs, he convinced me that if you cut their legs off and then threw their bodies back into the river, they would grow new legs. I was three years old at the time and believed my dad's heinous lie; that is, until this particular night in 1968.

As we approached a man poised silently with his gig held high above his head, I watched in horror as he speared a frog and, after quickly severing its legs, threw its body into a trash can. I went ballistic, waving my arms wildly while tottering with my full baby-belly on a twisted old tree trunk that was rising surreptitiously out of the river. As I lambasted him for not throwing the frog back into the river so that it could grow new legs, my husband's friend began to laugh so hard he rolled backward and nearly landed in the river himself! Obviously, I was no longer going to be a participant in this dangerous and now-lethal sport. My beleaguered husband decided to accompany me back to the road, where we would wait for the others in the comfort of our pick-up truck. Why we didn't decide to just go home still remains a mystery. Maybe we both knew we were there for another reason . . .

As we approached the pick-up, I noticed a large weeping willow tree on the other side of the road. As a kid, I had spent many hours playing under the lush canopy of the weeping willow that my dad had planted in our backyard. Years later, on this mystical night, my husband and I crossed the street and parted the weeping willow's ground-sweeping fronds, stepping through them as though they were a doorway into a giant green tent. Neither of us spoke during this experience and to this day we have not discussed the events of that night.

It was pitch-black inside the tree's canopy. All around, the willow's branches touched the ground, blocking out any moonlight. I could barely see the trunk in the center of the tree's interior, yet something compelled me to climb down the precarious four steps off the embankment and into the tree's cavernous space. My husband followed silently. Once inside, we moved slowly toward the center until we stood next to the trunk. The tree was huge. I marveled at its size, imagining children using it as a playhouse. Suddenly, a sound rose up from the ground below the branches directly in front of us. It was a rattlesnake. I believe that certain sounds awaken a primordial awareness of life-threatening danger in all of us, regardless of our age or experience. The rattle of a rattlesnake is one of those sounds. The moment it began I shifted my upper body, without moving my feet, an inch or two backward. Instantly, rattling began directly behind us. Again, I shifted my weight, this time toward the road, thinking it must be safe as we had entered from that direction. No such luck. The area instantly filled with the sound of rattling, merging with the deafening rattling from both in front of and behind us. At this point, I shifted toward the tree's trunk and the direction toward the other side of the trunk. Incredibly, this move was also met with shaking rattles. Now, the entire space under the giant weeping-willow tree was filled with a cacophony of shaking rattles, completely surrounding us in all directions. We had stepped into a rattlesnake den. We were about to die, and we knew it. All of this time, my husband was still standing next to me. Our movements and thoughts, I believe, were in unison. However, since we've never spoken of this night, I'm not sure if the following pertains to him also. The rest of this experience was extremely personal for me.

While quickly becoming aware that my life was about to end, I noticed that, instead of primordial fear, the following thoughts were beginning to move through my mind and consciousness. As time seemed to slow to a crawl, and as the frightening number of rattlesnakes were still shaking their dire death warning, it occurred to me that even though I was prepared to die, it didn't seem fair that my baby wouldn't have a chance to experience life in this world. I was an adult and had lived a somewhat full, though still very short, life. At home, we had a beautiful toddler daughter, Laura, who would undoubtedly be raised by my mother, as both of her parents were about to be goners. It didn't make sense to me, however, that I had carried this baby to full-term only to have him die with me. I had always had a feeling that my children would someday be a catalyst for some type of healing in our world.

With that last thought, my entire experience shifted to a completely altered and outrageously unbelievable one, something that I would have a lot of trouble believing if I were to hear it from someone else. But the events were exactly as I am about to describe them, and at no time will I add to the truth. To do so would invalidate everything I am trying to accomplish, which is to help you to restore your memory of being *Home with God*. So I hope that you can wrap your mind around this. Here goes . . .

While standing under the giant weeping willow tree, completely surrounded by a den of hissing and rattle-shaking rattlesnakes, I suddenly find myself encapsulated within a brilliant white tube, or tunnel, of about seven feet in diameter and of seemingly endless length. Somehow, I know that this tube connects everything that exists on earth—the trees, oceans, mountains, valleys, and all of Life. It identifies itself to me as "*One.*" Within this tube of *One,* I become *one* with everything, experiencing myself as a part of all existence in a field of benevolence that even houses the snakes who had been threatening to end my life just a moment before. The very instant I enter the undulating tube of *One,* however, the snakes' cacophony of rattling stops. I become aware that I can speak to them as I hear a voice that is exquisite in its tone coming from my lips, "*Your home is lovely. I mean you no harm. I am with child.*" In unison, the rattlesnakes reply in an equally melodic, but more masculine, tone, "*We can see that. We mean you no harm. Go out the way you came in.*" As instantly as it had appeared, the tube of *One* is gone. I turn to my husband and motion toward the exit. We retrace our footsteps, very carefully, back out of the den and up onto the road. No rattles shake. Once on the street, we stop and look up toward the moon. It is full. As I gaze at the moon, I know that my life will never be the same again . . .

# The Tone

I can hear God speaking
By listening to the tone
of your voice
Every sound you make,
every secret you whisper
Every opinion you declare
Speaks from Spirit
Even those utterances
flavored by attitude
Those intricate nuances,
your voiceprints

I can feel God's feelings
By hearing the words
you long to speak
Slipped in between the syllables
of your judgments
As you tell me how you feel
What you fear, why you cry,
How you dread the way you feel
when you speak
Unaware you speak for all

I can touch God's heart
By feeling the compassion
in the tone of your voice
As you strive to speak in harmony
With the memory of the sound
Of who you are

# NEAR DEATH

A period of accepting and settling usually occurs after a person experiences an event that defies understanding. In my case, the willow tree experience—although leaving a deep and profound impact on me—needed to be put away for a while so that I could devote myself to my young family. I was reluctant to tell my family and friends about the experience until I came across a story by a young psychology graduate named Raymond Moody. Dr. Moody had just written *Life After Life*, a recounting of near death experiences, or NDEs, as reported by patients who had been declared clinically dead for a period of approximately four minutes. Of the NDE experiences reported to Dr. Moody, a series of five events came to be known as "common denominators." The first common denominator involved the patient becoming aware of him or herself outside of his or her body, usually floating in the air above or in a corner of the room. The second common denominator involved being met by a deceased loved one or relative. The third involved being escorted through a tunnel toward a light. This caught my attention! Although I hadn't been injured and/or declared clinically dead, I had entered a tunnel (the tube of *One*) that ascended my reality to one of a higher level of existence. The remaining two common denominators involved a past-life review and then a return to the corporeal body.

*Life After Life* was followed by *Life Before Life*, Dr. Moody's response to the vast number of readers who contacted him after reading his earlier work. In *Life Before Life*, Dr. Moody regresses patients to the period before they were born, with astounding results. Since then, Dr. Moody has written several additional books detailing his ongoing work with people who have experienced alternate levels of existence. I highly recommend reading any or all of his enlightening material, especially if you've had a spiritual experience yourself. My personal favorite of his books is *The Reunion*.

Since my first voyage into the tube of *One,* I have entered the tunnel and traveled to varying locations on the *other side* to what I call "alternate dimensions of reality" innumerable times, some of which I will describe in this book. However enlightening experiencing the many other alternate dimensions of reality may be, though, they are still on *this* side of the esoteric border between *Home with God* and here. Alternate realms are actually very easy to visit. We do it often as we sleep. The missing element for most people is *consciousness.* Once you learn to reconnect your waking consciousness to your multi-dimensional spirit, or your higher consciousness, you will not only be able to consciously access higher realms of alternate dimensions of existence, you'll very possibly achieve the ultimate goal we've established for you in this book—a fully awakened (conscious) state of being *Home with God . . .*

# The Gift

*If I were allowed to give*
*just one gift*
*I would give it to you*
*If my gift were one of touch*
*I'd stroke you cheek and hair*
*If my gift were one of sound*
*I'd whisper your name in your ear*
*If my gift were one of time*
*I would give you Now*
*If my gift were one of sight*
*You would behold eternity*
*through a child's eye*
*If my gift were one of feeling*
*You would bask in Peace*
*If my gift were one of teaching*
*I would instruct you to wake up*
*You've been asleep*

# THE SPICE RACK

In my teens and twenties, I suffered from recurring upper respiratory infections which often developed into laryngitis or bronchitis. As a child, shortly after my father passed away, I developed a severe case of tonsillitis that failed to respond to antibiotics. At the same time, I developed an allergic reaction to the antibiotics and it was decided that we would wait a while before removing my tonsils. During the wait, however, my body absorbed my tonsils! My doctor had been away on a long trip to Europe and, upon his return, he examined my throat and exclaimed in surprise that my tonsils had been removed! Actually, they had been somehow absorbed into my system! I had been in bed for weeks, writing with a chalk board because I couldn't speak, trying to tell my family that my tonsils had turned into cork in my throat until they had finally dissolved and disappeared altogether.

Although I no longer had symptoms of tonsillitis, I continued to go down with sore throats, laryngitis and bronchitis every winter, sometimes even in the summer. As a young mother, this trend continued until I was diagnosed at 22 with a fast-growing tumor in my throat. Because the tumor was tangled up with my larynx, or vocal cords, my doctor, who was also a surgeon, was going to have to remove them along with the tumor. Upon hearing this news, I had a visual flash of myself *speaking to small groups of people in my middle years.* Apparently, I had something important to say to them and I wouldn't be able to do it if I couldn't talk. I asked to delay the surgery for a few weeks. My doctor, thinking I had lost my mind, reluctantly agreed, asking me why I would risk waiting any length of time before having the surgery. I explained, "I grew this thing. Maybe I can un-grow it!"

A light flashed over his head as he, looking surprised, exclaimed, "By golly, Janet! I think you can do that!"

Later that morning, alone at home, I looked up to the ceiling and said, "OK, God, You've got my attention. I've been away for a long time but I'm back now and I'll never leave You again. I need to know why I grew this thing and I need to know how I can get rid of it." At that moment, reality suspended itself for the third time in my life and I heard an indescribably beautiful voice speak to me with these words, "*Go to your spice rack.*" I was dumbfounded. For years, I had been openly rude to "health nuts" and people who believed that weeds (herbs) could have any kind of therapeutic effect on their physical body or their health. Now, when being faced with my own health crisis, I'm being told that something in my *spice rack* will heal my illness! And here's the *really* weird thing—until two weeks before, I had never even owned a spice rack!

It had been a gift, given to me at the surprise housewarming party my family and friends held for me a couple of months after my husband and I had purchased our first home. Everyone was in the dining room gathered around the cake and the gifts, which were piled on top of the dining room table. I had gone into the kitchen to make a pot of coffee to go with the cake. (At this point, I was still completely unaware that a fast-growing tumor was percolating in my throat. I had no symptoms other than an overactive thyroid, which was also entangled with the tumor.) Suddenly, a beautiful young woman appeared, seemingly out of nowhere, holding a package. She was blond, with translucent skin, and she smiled at me as though she had known me forever.

"Hi! Here, I brought you a gift," she exclaimed, handing the wrapped package to me.

I stammered, accepting the gift, and motioned toward the dining room, saying "Thank you! Let's go put it on the table with the others." I really wanted to get her into the dining room so that whoever had brought her to the party could introduce us. Even though she apparently knew me, I had never seen her before in my life.

She shook her head, smiling, "No. I want you to open it now, please."

Baffled, I agreed and removed the wrapping. It was a spice rack. It looked just like the kind I had seen in my friends' kitchens, hanging on the wall over their stoves. I turned toward my stove and placed the spice rack on the upper ledge, where it fit perfectly. Never expecting to use the spices in it since I had always seasoned my food only with salt, pepper, paprika and "Dixie Fry," (my mom had been raised in the South, where Cajun seasonings ruled,) I thought it might at least be a pretty décor item my kitchen. Turning back to my mysterious guest, I was startled to find her gone. I searched throughout the house, asking everyone where she had gone. *No one else had seen her or even knew of her!* It took me almost thirty years to figure out that my beautiful guest with the spice rack was an angel, bringing me the medicine that I would need in just a couple of weeks . . .

So now, two weeks later and in dire need of healing, having just been told by the *voice* to go to my spice rack, I have found a new thrust of faith in God and in natural health, quickly realizing that I would need to apologize to almost everyone I knew for all of the times I had rudely dismissed their enthusiasm about herbs and anything natural. It was the early 1970s and young hippies and naturalists were wearing long ponytails and exclaiming, "You are what you eat." (Little did I know that someday I would be the director of a school of natural health and be *speaking to small groups of people in my middle years* on that very same concept.)

So now, with my newfound confidence, I selected what I *felt* were the precise spices and herbs for my purpose—cinnamon, cloves, nutmeg, ginger and thyme. Except for the thyme, the first four spices have been used in Eastern Indian Ayurvedic medicine as a natural health tonic since antiquity. It's called chai tea and is widely available today in grocery stores, health food stores and coffee houses. Of course, back then I had never heard of it. Nor had I heard of aromatherapy, an ancient method of healing with the essential oils of specific plants and flowers, including the five I had just selected from my spice rack that morning so many years ago. Once I had the bottles uncapped, I put on a teapot of water to boil.

Enthusiastically hoping for a powerful healing, I placed a half teaspoon of each spice into a mug. Then, as I poured the boiling water over the powders, the steam began to rise with an exquisite aroma. I picked up the mug and prepared to drink the thick steaming brew, but stopped when the *voice* instructed, "*No . . . no . . . no . . . Don't drink it. Breathe it.*" Grabbing a kitchen towel, I threw it over my head to capture the steam and, holding the mug to my lips, began inhaling the vapors as though my life depended on it. (Hmm. I think it did!) I was unwittingly engaging in aromatherapy, a practice that is now sweeping the world in popularity. Instinctively, I knew that I would somehow heal from this simple act. I repeated the process every day for five days and then returned to my doctor for a recheck of the tumor's size. It had shrunk by half! Over the next six weeks, it disappeared entirely, and has never returned.

After this miraculous healing in 1972, I embarked on a study of all things natural, finally enrolling in a post-secondary school of natural health in Scottsdale, Arizona. Today, I have my own post-secondary school of natural health and have published a book on holistic nutrition called *FigureShaping—The Completely Natural Weight-Loss Protocol*, which I originally wrote in 1991 and revised in 2007, adding a new chapter on *Nutri-Escience—The Science of Essential Nutrition*, which introduces several newly-discovered advances in natural medicine. Throughout the entire time I have been studying and working in the natural health field, however, the main focus and emphasis of my personal and professional life has been to experience and to share the more spiritual aspect of health and wellness, which all too often is neglected when approaching the "holistic" model of healing. This model embodies the term "mind/body/spirit," which embraces and utilizes a wide variety of natural healing techniques that are, for the most part, designed to heal through accelerating frequency. One of the benefits of accelerating our frequency is that we are more likely to experience ourselves with our higher awareness, or spiritual consciousness, and one day find ourselves, maybe for just a moment or two, bathed in the infinite light and indescribable love of being *Home with God* . . .

# Joe

*I know who'll greet me first*
*When the gate to heaven opens*
*Before parents who've waited*
*For forty years*
*And friends who never said goodbye*
*It will be Joe*

*Joe, short for Bo Joe*
*Short for Bo Jangles*
*A rescued springer*
*who captured my heart*
*And, yes, after twenty years*
*I still grieve*
*Which is why I know*
*It will be Joe*

*He'll knock me down*
*And lick the stars off my face*
*And cry with me*

*He'll leap higher than he did*
*Before his gait slowed*
*And he'll wiggle his freckled rear*
*And flounce his floppy ears*

*And while Joe and I tumble to the grass*
*I'll catch a glimpse of your faces*
*Wide with grins and wet with tears*
*Waiting patiently*
*To welcome me Home*
*But I know who'll be first in line*
*It will be Joe*

# THE HIDDEN VALLEY

For three years after my unorthodox throat-tumor healing, I studied every piece of literature I could get my hands on that related to natural health, especially if it concerned spices and herbs. At the same time, I quested for books by spiritual authors, looking for methods to rekindle my esoteric experiences as often as possible. In 1975, while looking through my mother's bookshelf, I came upon a hard-cover volume by Vernon Howard called *The Mystic Path To Cosmic Power*. The name sounded a little "out there" to me but something about the *energetic feel* of the text itself convinced me to take it home.

To this day, I can still feel the book's cover in my hands. It was silver, with a brocade-type texture. I read throughout the day and night, devouring the simple yet profound truths it shared. At one point while reading the book, I laid it, open, on my chest and fell asleep. During my nap, I became conscious and aware that I was as light as air and that I was being lifted up and cradled in what felt to me like enormous golden arms. To this day, I have never felt so *comforted* in my life. I believe those golden arms provided my first glimpse of being *Home with God*. I was 25 years old.

That same year, I experienced my first dream/OBE (Out of Body Experience). It was early morning, about 7:30, and I was sleeping peacefully when I suddenly became consciously aware that I was sleeping in my bed and was also in *another* place, and I was experiencing this other place with a vivid, wakeful state of mind that felt more real than my everyday life had ever felt. I remember thinking, "*This is more real than reality!*"

In this *other place*, I was precariously climbing rock ledges inside the interior wall of a huge cavern, moving methodically and laboriously toward a light that was streaming in through an opening near the top of the cave. Each step was treacherous, and I had to fumble for the ledges one at a time, as I couldn't see the cave's interior well enough to map out my entire ascent. Finally reaching the light, I stepped through a doorway into a brilliant hidden valley, rimmed with mountains in the distance and banked by a stream running alongside its meadow. Birds dipped down to me and asked if I wanted to fly with them. I easily rose into the sky and flew with the birds, soaring effortlessly over the brilliant meadows. Then, touching down, I walked through the gardens. I vividly remember seeing my own hand as it touched the velvety flowers and felt their texture. As the birds flew away, I dove into the stream and swam underwater the entire length of the valley. Coming out of the water, I realized that I was not at all wet as I climbed up and onto a green lawn to discover *my house* sitting on the riverbank.

It was made of flowers—chrysanthemums, roses, daisies,—all in brilliant colors. Even the furniture was made of flowers! After strolling through each room and touching the kitchen countertops, which were also made of flower petals, I left the house and walked around to the rear of the building, feeling the need to see if the entire house was made of flowers. Amazed, I saw that it was.

At that point, I re-entered my sleeping body and awakened to this dimension. Grabbing a pen and note-pad, I wrote the entire experience down as a poem called *"The Hidden Valley."* Twenty years later, while studying English literature in college as part of a pre-requisite program toward acupuncture school, I re-wrote the poem in proper verse. I still don't know which version I like best. Here's the first . . .

# The Hidden Valley

It's a long, long road to the valley; her beauty is hidden from view
And the colors of her meadows are seen by very few
A dark cave looms before her, enshrouding those below
Who journey into Waiting, where only visions grow

In seeing all behind me, and knowing where I'm from
I turn my back on daylight and pray to find the sun
I step into the darkness alone and unaware
And I guide myself with memories of yesterday's despair

My search is nearly over; I see a radiant light
Filtered through a clearing in the shadows of the night
A gentle calm compels me to step beyond the door
Into a lustrous garden more magnificent than lore

Fragrant crimson roses and honeysuckle bend
Gently over the riverbank, dancing in the wind
Across the distant meadow, splendid in her glow
Beneath a misty rainbow stands my castle in the snow

I touch the velvet flowers; I join the birds in flight
Then I plunge into the river and drift into the night
I have seen the hidden valley; I have slept upon her loam
The truth is mine forever; the beauty is my own

And the second:

## The Hidden Valley

I stepped into a valley long ago
Of hidden beauty lush with velvet lawn
And meadows rising up to meet the dawn
Of dancing sunbeams whispering "Hello"

Honeysuckle beckoned on the breeze
As murmurs sprinkled gently from the sky
In droplets of an ancient echo cry
That stilled my heart and sent me to my knees

On wings of air I joined the birds in flight
And soared above a mountain capped with snow
Diving without fear into the night
Unaware of knowing what I know

Often still I wander on this loam
In the distant memory of *Home* . . .

# THE CALLING

The next few years brought many changes to my family's life. My marriage of 14 years had ended and my children and I began the first of what were to be many moves around the country. I was now enmeshed in the fitness and weight-loss industry, supervising 11 California figure salons. When the company was sold to an upstart diet company that did away with our healthy protocols and substituted them with a bevy of artificial diet foods, I resigned. In 1984, at age 33, remarried and living in New Jersey, I found myself in an emotional turmoil one fall afternoon.

I was cleaning my stove (hmm . . . that stove thing again . . .) and feeling extreme frustration that I had spent my entire life preparing for something to offer to the world as my contribution, or calling, and yet here I was—unemployed and not knowing how to focus my energy. I thought about the years I had spent studying creative writing after high school. As a kid, I had always planned to be a writer, but my life seemed to revolve around people and I erroneously thought writing would be a solitary avocation. My thoughts began to swirl, merging the recalling of my past into a sort of menagerie of passions—writing, natural health, esoteric studies . . .

Suddenly, a voice spoke into my ear, *"You will be a doctor."*

"What?" I shot back, paying little attention to the fact that someone was speaking to me again out of thin air. "I'm too old for medical school! And besides, I use natural medicine more than traditional."

*"Do the book thing."* This was directed from the *voice within*, but it was still coming from *Him*. I closed my eyes, entered the den where at least fifty books were housed in varying locations, and laid my hand on a book on the first try. Without opening my eyes, I picked up the book, opened it, and placed my index finger on one of the pages with absolute determination. Whatever passage it revealed, I knew would contain a message. The book was actually "Prevention" magazine. The line I placed my finger on read, "Become a Doctor of Natural Health," followed by a phone number. I called and enrolled on the spot.

Instead of waiting until my training was complete, I attended an internship at the institute before beginning my studies, which were applied through distance learning. As a novice, I watched while the graduating students received their diplomas. On my flight home from the campus in Arizona, I felt like I was soaring higher than the airplane! Something huge and wonderful was happening and I had no idea what it was! Little did I know that I was feeling the magnificence of *spirit* surging through my physical body simply because I had said *yes* to this new adventure. The ball was beginning to roll and I was completely unaware of how much ground it would be covering. Once I reached home, however, I received a heart-stopping call from my friend, Patti . . .

# Words of Spirit

Words of Spirit can heal
They reach into your heart
And tie a love-knot
Made of brilliant light
Reaching like a strand of lace
As it shimmers into the heart
Of everyone you know

Words of Spirit can uplift
Helping us to remember our gifts
To humanity and to ourselves
The actions of our hearts
Put away so long ago
Until we call them back
Into being

Words of Spirit can inspire
Enabling us to begin
The ultimate task of love
Creating our lives anew
As we look at every day
Every person, every event
With a clear choice
To give our highest moment
And receive our highest honor
In love expressed
With words of Spirit

# PATTI GREER

Patti was a rare talent. She sang, with her band, in the upscale casino nightclubs of Atlantic City. My husband, a pianist, also played in the clubs. Patti and I became fast friends and I often watched her performances when she and my husband appeared on the same nights. Her voice was exquisite. At the age of 30, she had become well-known enough to catch the attention of a Hollywood producer, who invited her to Los Angeles to shoot a pilot for a sit-com about her life. While there, Patti was diagnosed with uterine cancer and, instead of filming the pilot, underwent surgery. Returning home, she was upbeat and hopeful for another chance for stardom in the future. Unfortunately, the cancer reappeared within months in her left lung.

Surgery was out of the question. If Patti lost a lung, she wouldn't be able to sing, and Patti lived to sing. She enrolled in a then-experimental program that was testing the effectiveness of a new chemotherapy drug. The drug is widely used today, with no small thanks to Patti, who was the first person to survive the drug's harsh side effects. While it was administered, she had to be watched closely throughout the night, so a hospital stay was essential. It was during one of those stays that I received the call from her.

It was 3:00 a.m. Patti was on the phone asking me to come to her bungalow on the beach and sit with her. I knew that she had driven over 40 miles to the hospital the night before for her injection and that she was supposed to have stayed there until morning. Something had to be wrong. I rushed to her cottage. She was lying on the couch, perfectly still. A tear fell from her cheek as she explained to me why she had slipped out of the hospital during the nurses' shift change at midnight, "My heart hurts."

I immediately thought the injection had somehow missed her lung and penetrated her heart. "Did the needle slip?"

She smiled, "No, you nut. Frank broke up with me." Frank was my husband's drummer. He and Patti were engaged. Recently, Frank had lost his mother to cancer and was now clearly unable to go through this ordeal with Patti. He had ended it that night. I was dumb-struck. I had no idea how to help my friend heal from a broken heart. I felt helpless.

"You know that thing you do with your hands?" she asked softly.

When I was a young girl I had occasionally been asked to do the "laying on of hands," a spiritual healing technique my mother was convinced I was "gifted" with. The subject came up very rarely and most people didn't even know I had this "gift." As I got older, I realized that spiritual healing was considered taboo in our culture and I quickly dropped the practice, that is, until these many years later when Patti, returning from Los Angeles, told me she had been diagnosed with lung cancer. Without thinking, I had suggested to her that I might do the "laying on of hands" to help her with her healing. She had looked at me like I was from another planet, "No, that's OK. I'll just go the medical route." She had backed away from me slightly when she said this. Mortified, I vowed that I would never bring up the subject again. For eighteen months, Patti had undergone bi-monthly injections of chemotherapy that, so far, no one else had survived. The cancer, however, kept reappearing in another spot. Thankfully, it was only in one side of her lung. I think she would have continued with the chemotherapy injections had her heart not been broken that fateful night. But how could my "laying on of hands" now help heal her broken heart?

"I don't know how to fix your heart!" I stammered.

"Not my heart." Patti shook her head slowly, "Only time can heal that. I want you to do your hands thing for my lungs." Her eyes were closed. They had been closed since I had arrived at her cottage.

"I thought you were only going the medical route." I was wide-eyed.

"Not anymore. I'm never going back to that hospital. It's not helping me anyway."

I should have panicked. This was a tall order for a lady who didn't even know if she still had the "gift." But something told me not to worry. I knelt next to the couch and began to wave my hand over her body in a slow sweeping motion, as though I was scanning her energy field.

Patti asked, "What are you going to do?"

I shrugged, "I don't know." This healing wasn't in my hands. I knew that any healing would come from God, and that I was just a conduit for His Healing Energy to move through. I scanned her lungs until I found a cold spot, then gathered energy from the air in the room around us and concentrated it in my hands. Placing one hand over the other, I laid them directly over the cold spot on Patti's chest and, sitting on my heels, remained motionless for about 15 minutes. During that time, events occurred in that little cottage on the beach that I still consider flabbergasting. But I was there. Patti and I both witnessed it, and we're both still here to tell you about it.

The room was softly lit from a lamp on the far left. The couch was just under a window that looked out over the sandy beach and the Atlantic Ocean. It was pitch black outside. There was a calm silence, which was enhanced by the hypnotic rolling of ocean waves in the background. Within a minute or two, I noticed a flicker of light across the room, near the ceiling. I thought it was a firefly, although I had never seen a firefly before and didn't even know if they were found in this part of the country. Immediately, another flicker occurred, then another. Within a short time, the entire corner of the room was illuminated with tiny flickering lights. Suddenly, the corner of the room near the ceiling directly above us began to light up with tiny flickering lights. Then the corner behind us lit up and, last, the corner opposite. All at once, thousands of tiny flickering lights began to spread throughout the entire ceiling, illuminating the room brightly. Patti opened her eyes and, without moving her head, shifted her gaze from one side of the ceiling to the other, watching the flickering light-show.

I looked at her and whispered, "Do you see that?"

"Mm-hum," she murmured, closing her eyes peacefully, with a hint of a smile on her lips. I continued to watch the flickering lights in fascination until my attention was suddenly diverted.

It was as though someone I couldn't see had pulled up a step ladder right in front of me and climbed up onto it with a "Mary, Mary, quite contrary" watering pitcher outfitted with a fine mesh screen, and began to pour a mist of cool water down over my head. The water came from above me, not inside of me, so I knew it wasn't sweat. It continued to pour over me until I was drenching wet, even the insides of my shoes. The mist rained only onto me. Patti didn't get wet at all. The shower continued for about five minutes and then abruptly stopped. At that same moment I knew that Patti's healing session was complete and I lifted my hands from her chest. Simultaneously, she sat bolt upright and declared, "I'm hungry. Let's order a pizza!" Casino towns usually have all-night pizza delivery. We ordered a large pizza and Patti ate almost the entire thing by herself! This was very unusual since a common side effect of her chemotherapy was nausea and loss of appetite. I knew somehow that God had blessed Patti with a complete healing that night.

Several months later when I attended a debut of her new show, Patti asked me to stand as she told the sold-out audience of 1,500 people that I had saved her life. Slightly embarrassed, I stood there hoping they thought that I had perhaps pushed her out of the way of an oncoming train. I was still reluctant to admit that I had participated in a spiritual healing.

During the next few years, I busied myself with my natural health studies and then, one afternoon while sitting in my hairdresser's chair, I first heard the word that resonated throughout my body, mind, and soul with instant recognition—"Reiki." I knew immediately that Reiki was one and the same as the laying on of hands that I had instinctively done as a child and with Patti. Although I decided instantly to study Reiki, it would be six more years before I would finally find myself in the presence of my Reiki instructor. In the meantime, a few other lessons were in store for me.

# The Loved Child

Tell your child you love him
Every solitary day
Every single conversation
Regardless of its tone
If you speak from your heart
You will speak the truth
Even with the angst, the spitfire
The mirroring of peers
Love prevails

To give him that
To let him know he is loved
At all times, at every moment
Can free his mind and heart
From doubt of his worth
The boldest menace to life

For years we staged a standoff
Concerned we'd feed them
Too much icing
Forgetting that the batter's
Main sustenance
Is the love ingredient
That nurtures his soul
While icing only decorates

How many days do we wait
To tell them that we love them?
A starving child knows fear
Love can move mountains
But fear can move a small finger
Over a trigger

# THE COURTROOM

It was 1985. I was visiting my mother and sister at their home in California when tragedy struck. My sister, Darleen, and I were driving to a neighboring town for dinner when we encountered an ambulance heading in the opposite direction. We exchanged glances. Somehow, we knew that someone in our family was in trouble. Thus I found myself, weeks later, sitting in a courtroom with my younger brother, waiting for his case to be heard. He was charged with involuntary manslaughter from an accident involving his motorcycle. As bad as that was, he was not in custody. We were there for his arraignment.

As we sat on the right side of the courtroom, we watched as eight men in orange jumpsuits, with their hands and feet secured in chains and locks, were escorted, one by one, into the room and seated on the left, opposite us. I had never seen a prisoner in chains before, much less eight prisoners, and I worried that we would have to wait until all of their cases were heard before my brother's turn came up. Sure enough, they began to call the men to appear before the judge, one at a time. The first to be heard was a thin, scraggly young man with dark blond hair and a patchy beard. He was about 24 years old. He kept his head bowed, lifting it only to answer the judge with, "Yes, your honor," as each charge was read. I watched him intently, wondering why this young man had gone down the road of criminal behavior that was now probably going to cost him many years of his life serving time in prison, not to mention the lifetime of anguish his actions may have visited upon his victim.

As I contemplated the young man's plight, I realized that I was not judging him—something that I was always pretty sure I would do if I ever came face to face with a man being charged with his crime—especially as he appeared to be admitting his guilt. I looked around the room at the other spectators and wondered if any of them were passing judgment and condemnation on this man for his behavior. All faces were blank, without emotion of any kind. I looked back at the young man and began to wonder about his life; what could have brought him to this despicable behavior. As I watched him, I began to imagine him as a young child—a toddler of about two years old in his mother's kitchen. Although I didn't see his mother in my mind's eye, I imagined her in the room with him, looking down at him and speaking to him. As I gazed at him, these thoughts occurred to me, "*I wonder if maybe he was a victim, too. Maybe he was deeply wounded when he was a small child. I wonder if his mother . . .*" At that very instant, the entire scene was transformed into one of the most profound and exhilarating experiences of my life, even to this day.

Four indescribable events occurred simultaneously, all of them taking place in less than ten seconds. The first was a sensation of *exquisite joy and peace* that rose up from the base of my spine, moving throughout my entire body and expanding outward for several feet. Second, with this blissful movement and presence of infinite joy, I became filled with a *rainbow of brilliant colors* cascading throughout my entire being. Third, I could hear a choir of angelic song and ethereal music, *coming from someplace vast within me*, that bathed everything in eternal peace. Last, but as all of these events took place at the same time—simultaneously—these four sentences, directed at the young man before the court, moved through me and out of my lips, audible only to me from within, "*You are My son. I forgive you. I love you. I am Jesus.*" The sentences were not spoken in my voice, but in the voice of Christ. *(I am crying as I write this. My deepest prayer and strongest desire is that every human on earth is blessed with this experience, for nothing in our world can compare to being filled, even for a second, with the Holy Spirit of Christ.)*

The effect on me from this experience was so great that I burst into tears. The judge halted the proceedings and stared intently at me until I composed myself. He must have thought that I was one of the young man's victims or a family member. Everyone in the courtroom was staring at me, even the young man who had just received Jesus' blessing. My brother was trying to console me, thinking I was distraught about his case. I managed to compose myself and remain silent while the rest of the young man's charges were rendered. Finally, the judge was finished with him and he was escorted out of the courtroom.

The next prisoner to face the judge was a burly, dark-haired man in his thirties. As I watched him, I was sure that I could never be the conduit for another of Christ's blessings if he was to be the recipient. I quickly decided that he was someone I definitely would not want to encounter in a dark alley. *Even though, he had once been a child . . .* As I gazed at him, I found my thoughts drifting to his childhood, envisioning him as a dark-haired, chubby little toddler in the kitchen. *I wondered if he, too, had been a victim, a wounded child. Maybe his mother . . .* Instantaneously, I was again filled with the entire experience of being enveloped by Christ. Infinite peace, rainbows of shimmering colors, ethereal music and, exquisitely, Christ's spoken words of His blessing, "*You are My son. I forgive you. I love you. I am Jesus,*" all moved through me exactly as before, only this time they were directed at this unsavory-looking character. I burst, once again, into tears. By now, everyone in the courtroom, including my brother and the judge, thought I was involved in some sort of nerve-wracking trauma. Apologizing profusely, I left the courtroom and waited for the rest of the afternoon outside.

As I sat near the courthouse, watching people on the street going about their daily lives, I tried to figure out why the word "*mother*" had instigated those deep and profound blessings from Christ for those two men, and why the blessings had been directed to them through *me*. Both of the men had been charged with crimes against women. I couldn't help but wonder if both of their mothers had been physically abusive to them as small children. Or maybe that some type of verbal or physical punishment, offered as discipline perhaps, could have affected them so severely as young children that they lashed out at women as adults. As for why Christ chose to move through me to offer His blessing of forgiveness to the men—I think I may have been the only one in the courtroom who was willing to see the criminals as victims, too. That simple contemplation may have rendered me unable to personally judge the men for their acts, which could have prevented me from conveying their blessing from Christ and from personally experiencing an uncommon and unforgettable gift of bliss . . .

It may appear from my obvious dedication to Christ that I had been raised in a fundamentally religious household. Actually, my upbringing was very eclectic, blending old-time religion with a more esoteric spiritualism. I can thank my own mother for that. She was a model of diplomacy, always allowing people to express their differences without animosity. She knew that all religions and spiritual beliefs had merit and were only trying to point in the same direction toward remembering our true relationship with our Creator. In that pursuit, my family attended just about every church in our small community. I loved Sunday School. The stories about Jesus that were taught to us in Sunday School were very intriguing to me. They often portrayed Him as a young man going through many of the same trials and tribulations that we in the modern world were faced with every day. But even as a small child, I knew that Jesus was different. No one taught me that. I instinctively knew that not only was He the *Son of God*; He was also *our Brother.* I also knew that *He speaks to all of us, all of the time.* Our ability to hear Him was dependant on our willingness to listen. It is true that we can know God when we are willing to meet Him halfway. Christ, I believe, is the *Bridge* that connects us to our Creator. And that the meeting ground is just a hair's breadth away, *within us,* in the realm of His and our one true reality—*Home with God* . . .

# *Whatever Is Given*

*Whatever is given*
*comes back to me*
*Seven times over*
*Laced with love or fear*
*Depending on what it is*
*That I have given to you*
*How many times in my life*
*Have I seen this truth demonstrated*
*In its pure magnificence*
*Of simplicity?*

*Whatever thoughts I entertain*
*Create my reality*
*Slowly or quickly*
*Depending upon the degree*
*Of contemplation*
*Composing their essence*
*I need only look around me*
*To see the magic of the mind*
*And the power of the heart*
*Instilled within everything*
*Everywhere, every moment*

*Whatever desire I choose to express*
*Draws to me that which I long for*
*Or that which I dread*
*Depending upon my willingness*
*To accept*
*Based upon my understanding*
*That I am entitled*
*Or to deny,*
*Based upon my belief*
*That I still need to withhold*
*The beauty of who I am*

# SCHOOL

I was now in my thirty-fifth year, and well on my way to a life of spiritual adventure. My day was still filled with the common events of running a household and raising a family. I also still labored as best I could over my natural health studies. Of course, I told no one about my sojourns into the realm of spirit. These experiences were far too personal to share and I was still afraid that no one would believe me. Over the years, as the experiences intensified, however, I began to share them with my closest friends and family members. It is they who have convinced me to finally write this book. Last summer, my sister, Darleen, said the magic words, originally spoken by Dr. Wayne Dyer, that brought me to the conclusion that it's now time for this story to be told: *"Janet, don't let your song die with you."* From that moment, I have been dedicated to bringing as much of my story to you as I can recall. Fortunately, spiritual experiences are registered in my memory much more clearly that normal, everyday events. *It's as though they are what is real and everything else is a dream. Hmm . . .*

The next five years were filled with studies, work, and more changes for my family. My marriage ended amicably after only three years, a casualty of mixed-family stress. My children were now in high school and college and I was working as a real estate agent for a resort developer in Brigantine, New Jersey, the coastal island where we lived. My natural health studies also stretched over those five years and my resort office always provided me with plenty of patients—co-workers who were willing to let me "practice" my herbal remedies on them during the cold-and-flu season. Eventually, I opened my own natural health center, offering bodywork modalities from six certified massage therapists, nutritional supplementation, wellness consultations, and my special area of expertise developed during the earlier years when I had worked as the supervisor for 11 California Gloria Marshall Figure Salons—a holistic weight-loss program.

The natural health school I attended via home-study carried its own line of nutritional supplements called Nutripathic Formulas. I utilized these formulas in my weight-loss program, combining them with the protocols I had learned while working with Gloria Marshall's Figure Salons. One afternoon I received a call from the founder of the school, Dr. Martin. I had been ordering large amounts of a select few products from his school's product line and he was curious as to why I relied so heavily on just those few items and nothing else. I explained that I was using specific Nutripathic Formulas for clients who were on my weight-loss program and that I was offering them at a discount if purchased in bulk. (This program is described in detail in my natural weight-loss book—"*Figure Shaping: The Completely Natural Weight-Loss Protocol.*") After I described the program to him, he asked me if I would allow him to share it with other natural health students enrolled at his school.

"Of course," I replied.

"What should we call it?" he asked.

"Well, I've always liked the term "*Weight Watchers,*" I offered.

"Then let's call it *Health Watchers.*"

The following month when the school's newsletter arrived detailing the new Health Watchers weight-loss program and giving credit to me as the co-developer I thought, "Hmm, this could be big. I should have asked for royalties." Instantly, I heard that now-familiar *voice* state firmly, "*Do not ask for a cent. You will be paid.*" I put the newsletter away and never gave it another thought. Nine years later, after moving back to California to care for my mother, who was ill, I *inherited* the school from Dr. Martin!

He had just sold Health Watchers to Puritan's Pride, a direct-sales vitamin supplement company based in New York. (You may have received one of their catalogs in the mail.) I had opened my new natural health center, the Holistic Life Center, the year before and, finding myself swamped with appointments, had just called him to see if he still had any mini-courses available. I wanted to book my full-day's ten clients all for the same three-hour timeframe, share a three-hour mini-course with them, and free myself from having to spend all day repeating myself to them one at a time. Incredibly, that very morning, Dr. Martin had decided to retire and, remembering how Health Watchers had been inspired, virtually *gave* his natural health school to me! Talk about getting *paid!*

# Magic

You have more magic in your little finger
That a whole wall of wisdom
You come from a place that manifests dreams
And turns them into a palpable crunch
Of feelings, textures and ideas
Springing up from your belly
Merging with your heart
And lunging into your throat
Where they either congeal into a lump
If you live in the land of Doubt
Or emerge as a song
If you dwell in Hope

Sometimes, you shout your magic
From the castle of vanity
Hoping the others will embrace
And give fire and credence to your dreams
While fearing you've given your power away
To unsuspecting thieves who haven't a clue
Your dreams are yours and yours alone

Be still, beloved
Your magic is real
Your voice, your cares, your worries
Are all part of the magic that is you
Wherever you choose to live

# CATCHING UP

1989. The resort development I had been working for since moving to the island six years earlier was beginning to run out of inventory and I considered moving, with the staff, to another resort development. My days were slowing down and I found myself with long stretches of time at the office. I was a loan officer for the property. I began to bring my spiritual books to work with me.

During this time, I operated my Brigantine health center in the mornings and then turned it over to my son's girlfriend for the afternoon while I worked at the resort loan office. My son, Steven, was attending junior college nearby and living at home with me. My older son, Michael, was enrolled at a chiropractic school in Georgia. My daughter, Laura, was a young wife and mother back home in California. Occasionally, we all got together for a family reunion on the island. Life was filled with potential. I hadn't shared much of my esoteric double-life with them at that point, however, because I wasn't sure how to explain something even I didn't understand. I just kept studying and reading, hoping for answers. Finally, a book fell into my hands that filled in some of the blanks.

In the 1970s, a writer named Richard Bach wrote a beautiful short book called *Jonathon Livingston Seagull*. It was an instant bestseller. While it was inspirational, its sequel, *Illusions,* was a giant leap into spirit! Richard then followed with *Bridge Across Forever* and then *One.* For a year, I read and re-read these books, desperately trying to ascertain whether Richard Bach was endowed with a wild imagination and wrote from it or if his stories could actually be based in truth. Even with my esoteric experiences, I couldn't imagine anything so outrageously improbable as the events he described. He introduced concepts that defied physical law as I understood it. Richard described a life of multi-dimensional experiences, time-travel, even an account of stopping time and rewriting an event that resulted in a different outcome! I was entrenched in pondering the possibilities.

About the same time, a Southern man with a giant hug named Dannion Brinkley wrote a spellbinding book called *Saved by The Light*. In it, Dannion tells of a near-death experience that lasted 28 minutes before he suddenly found himself alive again under a sheet on a stretcher in a hospital corridor, waiting to be escorted to the morgue. I absolutely loved the book. To this day, it is required reading material for students of my "Esoteric Studies" class at the institute. Since then, Dannion has written several additional books detailing his ongoing experiences with near-death. To date he has died, by his own testimony, four times. Each time, he has brought back almost unbelievable—but true, by all accounts—information to share with us. His most recent book, to my knowledge, is called *Secrets of the Light*. There is a copy on my living room coffee table as I write this.

I often visit with Dannion and his beautiful wife, Kathrine, whenever I attend a spiritual or natural health exposition in San Francisco or elsewhere in the Bay Area. Dannion is usually one of the featured speakers at these events. To check on his next speaking engagement and maybe get one of his famous hugs for yourself, go to www.dannion. com. Just being in his presence can send your frequency soaring. Dannion also organizes tours to the Mayan ruins and other sacred sites for spiritual adventurers. There was even a television movie made about his life called "*Saved by the Light*." I hope you enjoy his magnificent spirit and hearty laugh as much as I and millions of others have. If anyone deserves a place of honor on the halls of fame back *Home with God*, it's Dannion.

# Mother Loved You Best

*Did you know that Mother loved you best?*
*She took one look at your face when you were born*
*And knew she would always love you best*
*How could she not?*
*You charmed her with your flirtatious grin*
*Toothless, beguiling, trusting*
*Giving her permission to mold your mind*
*Into whatever she dreamt you would like to believe*
*As you ventured into the drama of life*
*She loved you so much she lived for you*
*She lied for you*
*She forgot for you*
*She died for you*
*She gave you everything she missed herself*
*And that was much more than you can ever know*

*You were in her every waking thought*
*Sleeping, too*
*Her need to protect you from harm*
*Was tantamount to the universe itself*
*She could do it, too*
*With the sheer will of her might*
*And the strength of her prayers*
*She forged a shield of protection*
*Made of unrelenting angels*
*To surround your every step*
*She told no one, perhaps a few*
*That she had commissioned this crew of fierce warriors*
*To clear the path for her child*
*For you*
*The one she loved the best*
*My sister, my child, my brother, my neighbor, my friend, myself*
*Her child, the one she loved the best*

# MOM

The segment about my mom is a book in itself. I've always wanted to tell her story to you but never realized until now how it could be framed within this text. Mom's story is actually woven into the tapestry of my lifetime of spiritual experiences over a 30-year period, so I'm going to present it throughout several segments here for clarity. The first segment will cover her history as it pertains to this work. The remaining segments will provide an almost unbelievable view of how, during the last five years of her life, my mother modeled for her family, for my school, and now for you, the depths of mastery a human can reach when choices for healing are made with intention. She was living proof of the power of having *the faith of a mustard seed* . . .

Mom was beautiful. She and my dad had a storybook life filled with family, friends, travel, and holidays. To Mom, family was paramount. After her children started coming, one every 18 months, she never worked outside of the home again. (She had run a small diner in the hills of West Virginia before she and Dad married and started a family.) Their first baby was a girl, Dorothy Joanne, named after their best friends, Dorothy (Dot) and Joseph (Joe). Mom and Dad and Dot and Joe were inseparable, even traveling together across the country to set down new roots in California. Most of my early childhood memories are of get-togethers with my parents, my siblings, and Dot and Joe, especially on holidays and vacations. When Dad died, however, our visits from Dot and Joe began to wane. It just wasn't the same anymore.

A widow at 35 with six children to raise, Mom must have been overwhelmed. Somehow, she managed to hide that fact from her children for most of the time. In those days, jobs for women were scarce, especially women over 30 and with a slew of kids. A widow with six children would need a new husband, but, of course, that would seem an impossibility. Who would step up to that? Well, actually, a couple of years later someone did. It was a rocky road for much of the time, but Mom and my step-father, Ray, married and had two more daughters.

We all carried on, moving through the usual paces of a family's day-to-day life. My sister, Dorothy, married after high school. I followed soon after. Around that time, Mom made a decision that would impact her health for the rest of her life. She traveled to Mexico and endured 21 injections of silicone in each of her breasts over the course of 21 days. In 1967, silicone implants were still in the trial stages, yet the news had been broadcast everywhere in the nation that soon women would be able to undergo a surgical procedure that would enhance their bust-line. Mom didn't want to wait. She had nursed eight babies and, at 43, was still strikingly beautiful. She just wanted to plump her boobies back up to a reasonable level. As a devoutly allopathic patient, she trusted modern medicine completely. It never occurred to her that a medical procedure, developed by modern science, could adversely affect her health, even if it was administered under suspicious circumstances.

In those days, we were very limited in our understanding of the effect that our diet and environment could have on our bodies and our ability to maintain an optimum level of wellness. Petro-chemicals were relatively unknown for their harmful effects, as they had been available to us for such a short time. Now, we know. Today's breast implants are filled with saline instead of silicone.

I'm still wary of advising my patients to have implants, however, because the pouch containing the saline is still made of synthetic materials and I believe that any quantity of petro-chemicals can have an adverse influence on our health. If we could just learn to love our bodies as they are, maybe we wouldn't be so driven to find ways to change them. If I could whisper one thing to all sleeping young women it would be, *"You are Perfect, Whole and Complete just as you are."*

When Mom returned from Mexico, she excitedly showed me her new plumped-up breasts. Even though I was only 17 years old, I had serious misgivings about Mom's news, however, finding myself filled with dread from the moment she whipped one of those new puppies out. Not wanting to dash her hopes nor minimize her joy, I just smiled and kept my thoughts to myself, mumbling as I left the room while slowly shaking my head, *"I don't have a good feeling about this . . ."* Her newfound buxom-beauty lasted all of three months. After that, she started to experience unusual discomfort in a previously extremely healthy body; so healthy, in fact, that she had never even had a dental cavity. Until now, my mother had never even complained of a headache! Over the next seven years, Mom suffered with unexplainable physical ailments, finally undergoing the first and second in a series of many surgeries.

First, her gallbladder had to be removed. It was practically calcified by the silicone that had made its way throughout her body. Since the silicone had been injected directly into her breast tissue and was not contained in pouches, it was able to travel freely and rapidly. After her surgery, I hoped that all of the silicone had been removed with the gallbladder. Her breasts were now back to their former saggy condition, so I knew it wasn't still contained there. Unfortunately, the damage to her body was only just beginning to become apparent. Within another year, her old incision scar from the cesarean-section birth of her youngest child had begun to bubble with a strange, gooey substance. The silicone was now in her uterus. Repeated attempts by her doctor to repair this condition failed. Finally, it was decided that she would need to undergo a hysterectomy.

I went to the hospital with her, expecting to be in the waiting room for what was supposed to be a one-and-a-half-hour surgical procedure. Instead, I waited for over seven hours until her surgeon met with me in the hallway outside of the operating room. Drenched in sweat, he was breathing so hard he could barely speak. I was terrified. He laboriously described my mother's surgery. After opening her up for a routine hysterectomy, he discovered that she had no bladder! He literally had to remove a layer of Mom's stomach and *sew* a new bladder for her! Coupled with the hysterectomy, her surgeries had taken *seven hours* to complete. He was baffled at how she had been able to function without a bladder. I'll never forget that brave surgeon. His father had been the founder of the hospital where he had just operated on my mother. He was only 42 years old. Two months later, he died in that same hallway of a massive heart attack. I've always wondered if my mother's surgery had shortened his life. There's not a shadow of a doubt in my mind that her bladder had been literally dissolved by the silicone.

Over the next 30 years, Mom had practically every major organ in her body repaired, replaced, or removed. She developed rheumatoid arthritis, diabetes, stroke, congestive heart failure and cancer, eventually undergoing an open-heart quadruple bypass surgery and, lastly, a double mastectomy. (The irony here is legion.) Throughout the last ten of those years she came close to death on several occasions, each time prompting me to take a leave of absence from my work and rush home to try to nurture her through her next crisis. In the interim, I lived and worked in some of the most beautiful areas of the Eastern Seaboard . . .

# The Light

*I saw the light again last night*
*Approaching slowly*
*Enveloping me in its glow*
*Expansive, all-consuming, everlasting*
*More gentle than a hummingbird's wing*

*It's a regular thing now, times of light*
*Since the day we met deep in the everglades*
*"Take the book," she insisted*
*The mysterious woman on the street*
*Her treasure, long awaited, unread*
*Must go with me for reasons yet hidden*

*Skepticism ruled, as doubt cast shadows on my face*
*Acceptance hinged on the trial*
*"It takes a lot to get through to you, doesn't it?"*
*The words played softly through my soul*
*Finally, validation*

The opening of a heart is an amazing thing to experience
First, the tremors, trepidation
Then, waves of shimmers, a few at a time
Radiant shimmers of joy
I slam the book closed, holding onto what I know
Yet needing more
I am secure in my anticipation
Without sleep, how would we ever awaken?

Vestiges of ego run deeper than the hidden caverns
But the pitfalls are the same
Loneliness, despair, darkness
Even a candle can anchor your step
Did you know that you have a candle in your heart?
Like the trick birthday candles
You can never blow this one out
It burns forever
Always has, always will
God struck the match

# THE LIGHT

In 1990, I transferred, along with some of my co-workers, to a new resort property in Florida. I thought I had died and gone to heaven. The Gulf coast of Florida was so beautiful that every day as I parked my car and walked across the street to the resort property on the beach, I thanked God for guiding me to this beautiful place. The resort was located on an island off the mainland of the West Florida coast of the Gulf of Mexico. Since reading "Once Upon an Island" in a Reader's Digest Condensed Book in my younger years, I have been fascinated with island life. I plan to retire someday to the island of Kaua'i, my favorite place on earth.

I had sold my natural health center in New Jersey before moving to Florida, deciding to just freelance occasional holistic health consultations while working for the marketing department of our new resort development so that I could spend some time enjoying my new home. I lived on the mainland and drove over a long bridge to work every day. My condo in Cape Coral was situated on one of the many canal waterways branching inland from the Gulf. Manatees would swim through the canals that banked the lush grounds behind the property. Small, private boats also trolled through those waterways. In the early morning hours just before the sun came up, I often woke to the sounds of fish jumping and splashing in the canal below my bedroom window. Had my mother not gotten so sick with pneumonia from one of her long bed-rests after another of her surgeries, I might be living in Florida still! I doubt that many folks leave once they've experienced *Xanth*. (*Xanth* is the name for Florida in a series of fantasy books by a wonderful author named Piers Anthony.)

Within a few months, our crew was transferred to a resort property near Disney World. Though I missed the Gulf's island resort and the carefree beach life, I loved visiting the theme parks in the Orlando area. I was surrounded by Disney World, EPCOT Center, MGM Studios, Sea World, Universal Studios, as well as Arabian Knights, Frontier Town, Gator-land, etc. This was like paradise for a 40-year-old perpetual teenager. As fun as my outward life was, though, it couldn't compare to the *"party within."* It was while working as a loan officer at one of our Orlando resort properties that I first encountered *"the light."*

One sunny afternoon while leaving my office and heading for the parking lot to my car, I noticed a woman walking down the sidewalk, about a hundred feet away. She caught my attention when she abruptly stopped in her tracks. Within seconds, she was standing directly in front of me. I sized her up immediately. She was well-dressed, wearing a two-piece suit and a long-strapped purse over her shoulder. Under her arm there was a small white bag. I figured she must be needing directions to one of the parks. She didn't look at all threatening.

The woman spoke to me in a question-like voice, "Please don't think I'm crazy!" she said, "I've been looking for this book for months" (motioning to the bag under her arm), "and I finally found a metaphysical book store down the street," (motioning toward a shopping area nearby), "and they ordered it for me. And now I'm so excited because they called me this morning and told me that it was in . . . and I just picked it up . . . and, well, I don't want any money for it," (shaking her head), "though I just paid $24 for it . . . but now," (exclaiming) "I'm being told that I have to give it to you!" With that, she thrust the white bag toward me. I was stunned.

"That's OK." I pushed the bag back toward her, thinking I must have encountered a real-life devotee from some weird religious cult who was going to try to hook me with written propaganda and then try to convince me to turn over the deed to my house. "You just keep your book and enjoy it."

I turned toward the lot where my car was parked and began walking toward it. I had about a half city block to travel. Instantly, the woman was walking alongside me, pleading with me to take the book.

"Please, you don't understand! Archangel Michael says you have to read it!"

"No, I do *not* have to read your book," I replied firmly. "You read it. Please, leave me alone." At this point, I'd begun to look around for someone to come to my rescue, but the lot was completely devoid of people. I mentally measured the distance to my car as compared to the distance from my office, thinking I might have to turn back to get away from this nutcase. She's talking about *archangels*, for God's sake! And now she's beginning to *cry*! I was much taller than she was, so I figured I could take her if I had to. I kept walking, ignoring her babbling, until I got to my car. Suddenly, she threw herself in front of my car's door and began pleading with me to take the book. "Stop!" I said, putting my palm up in a silencing motion. She froze, mid-word. Thinking, just in case, that I might be wrong about this weird encounter, I closed my eyes, faced the sky, and said, in a loud and impatient tone, "What?"

*"It takes a lot to get through to you, doesn't it?"*

Oh my God! It was *the voice*! I was being chastised by *the voice*! Quickly, I grabbed the bag and removed the book, apologizing to the woman, to Christ, to God, to the Archangels, to anyone and everyone I had offended with my rudeness and stupidity. Pulling off the bag, I looked at the cover of the book. It read, *The Star-Borne—Remembrance for the Awakened Ones*. The author's name was Solara. A sliver of my sarcastic edge returned as I thought, "Great! It's one of those woo-woo New Age books! Oh well, there must be *something* in here that I need to read." I flipped through a few of the pages, looking for some idea as to what it was that I needed to learn from this unorthodox material. Looking at the still frozen-silent woman, I asked, "Where can I find you in a week so I can give your book back to you?"

"I'll be right here," she promised. I gave her instructions to find my office inside the building and we parted company, both of us a little shell-shocked, I'm sure, by the strange events we had just experienced.

I drove to my next appointment at another office near Disney World. There, I settled in for a busy afternoon, but—you guessed it—not a single person approached my desk during my entire shift. I knew that I was being allowed a free day so that I could dive into the book. Turning to the first page, I read a couple of sentences. Suddenly, my heart exploded and imploded at the same time with a feeling of joyful anticipation that was amplified far beyond normal excitement. It was as though I was a child about to arrive on my birthday to the biggest party with the best gifts in the whole, wide world. I slammed the book shut. That much *happy* is hard to contain in one body. Slowly, I opened the book and read a few more sentences. Bang! More *happy!* This went on all afternoon and evening, until it was time to go home. Then, things got really interesting.

*I have now read into the night, finishing about half of the book by midnight. At this point, I'm too exhausted to read anymore. My "happy" bursts have finally subsided and I'm just meandering through the pages, amazed at the wonderful revelations in the text. I slowly reach over to my left and turn off the table lamp, resting the open book on my chest with my right hand still clutching it. The ceiling light is already off. My bedroom door is closed. The heavy drapes are drawn so tight that my bedroom is pitch black. I fall asleep, deeply. Suddenly, the light comes on. I awaken, startled. My eyes are still closed. I know that my room-mate, Robyn, is home, but I didn't hear her come into my room and turn on the light. She wouldn't do that anyway. Besides, this light is much brighter than my ceiling light. In fact, this light is so bright that I know I won't be able to open my eyes to it without burning them. It's as though someone has entered my room and is shining a giant, high-beam flashlight directly into my eyelids. The thing is, though, if you shine a light into your closed eyes, you'll see red, not white, because of the blood vessels. And this light is **brilliant white** . . . and all-encompassing.*

I pondered my dilemma for about a minute, then decided to face this intruder. For some unfathomable reason, I felt no fear. I opened my eyes. It was still pitch dark. I closed my eyes. Flash! The brilliant light was still on! I opened and closed my eyes a few times, stunned out of my mind by the strangeness of this experience. Each time, the light was on when I closed my eyes, and then it was off again when I opened them. Suddenly, within the brilliance of this all-encompassing light, there was an exhilarating celebration taking place. I was being greeted with a joyful barrage of singing, dancing and *Homecoming* congratulations from many, many very happy—*I don't know*—people? Angels? I couldn't *see* them. Everything was *light, everywhere!* But I could *feel* them, and I could feel their feelings of joy. It was indescribable.

After a few minutes, I felt that I couldn't endure this much joyful celebration any longer or I might shatter into a million pieces of bliss. So I said, *"Thank You! Now I know. I remember. Can we please turn off the lights now? I need to sleep."* Instantly, the light was extinguished. Exhilarated, yet exhausted, I fell immediately into a deep sleep. Within about a minute, the light came back on again, awakening me instantly. *"Just kidding!"* the celebrating voices exclaimed, as the light switched off again. To this day, unless I'm under a lot of physical or mental stress, which lowers my frequency, I receive a quick visit from *the gang in the light* most nights just as I am drifting off to sleep. I assume you have figured out by now that these visits are actually glimpses into *Home with God* . . .

A week later, when I tried to return the Star-Borne book to the mystery woman, she refused to take it. She stopped by my office to pick it up and found that she couldn't leave with it. Still, she wouldn't take any money from me. She just said that she would buy another one, as this one wanted to stay with me. That was over 20 years ago and the book is still with me. At this very moment, it is holding the space on a prayer ceremony in my kitchen, a practice I started a few weeks after receiving the book. Mom's doctor had called me late one afternoon and, explaining that Mom was desperately ill, suggested that I hop a red-eye to California. I grabbed a few things, including my Star-Borne book, and flew across the country that very night. Arriving at the hospital, I was shocked to see how white Mom's face was. She opened her eyes and saw me standing next to her in the intensive care unit. Immediately, color came back into her cheeks and lips. It was August, 1990, and Mom and I were about to embark on yet another journey guided by Spirit, one that would cover only a two-lane road . . .

# The Fairy

*Have you ever wondered if fairies were real*
*What they would look like?*
*If they glisten like a miniature star?*
*If their wings are like those of a butterfly?*
*If they dart about like Tinkerbelle*
*Or hover like a hummingbird?*

*Do they dance and spin in the air?*
*Or hide behind flower petals?*
*Are they shy?*
*Do they fear us as giants*
*When we trample their shelters?*
*Do they visit us at night*
*And sit on our shoulders*
*Sparkling?*
*Giving us praise when we honor*
*Their home, our home, Earth?*

*If I hoped that fairies were real*
*I'd invite one to visit me*
*As I sleep*
*Waking me with a soft brush of wing*
*Against my cheek*
*Dusting my pillow with tiny embers of light*
*As they spill from her radiance*

*I'd open my eyes slowly*
*So as not to frighten her; after all*
*She's only three inches tall*
*And I'd look into her smiling eyes*
*And whisper, "Thank you, too."*

# "ONE NEEDLE"

$M$om did so well over the next 24 hours that her doctor moved her to a regular patient room. This, however, was not enough for Mom. She wanted to leave the hospital and go home right away. Somehow, she convinced her doctor to release her to me. I packed her up and loaded everything into my car. We had just started for home when I found myself impulsively making a left turn into a parking lot across the street from the hospital. It was the parking lot for the patients of an acupuncturist, Dr. Dy. I had never visited this doctor before; I didn't even know if he was still in practice. I had only read a small article about him in the newspaper almost 15 years earlier that had announced his grand opening somewhere in this area. Back then, he was already in his 60s. How I knew that he was still in practice and that his office was located just across the street from the hospital is still a mystery to me. Where I got the audacity to just wheel my mom into his office without an appointment is even more of a mystery!

The front office was empty, except for an Asian woman, Dr. Dy's wife, behind the reception desk. I rolled Mom past her just like I knew what I was doing and headed down the hallway, turning into an office on the right. Dr. Dy was sitting behind his desk. He stared at us with wide, unblinking eyes. I rolled Mom up to his desk and, in effect, turned her over to him. Mrs. Dy rushed in behind us but her husband motioned for her to let us stay. I didn't speak. Dr. Dy looked into Mom's eyes and, with deep sadness and compassion, said, "I'm so sorry. I cannot help you. You are far too sick, ma'am." I hadn't realized how Mom's appearance might affect her chances of being treated. She had been wheel-chair bound for the past two years, massively crippled by rheumatoid arthritis. She could barely speak because of a misshapen neck that forced her chin to rest on her chest. Her contorted fingers were curled tightly, which rendered her hands unusable. Somehow, though, she was able to slowly and painfully uncurl her right index finger and point to her upper arm, saying in a barely audible voice, "One needle please, right here."

For years, Mom's pain, although general and severe, had been especially concentrated in her upper arms. She once said that it felt like someone was holding red-hot pokers against her arms. Without anti-inflammatory steroids, which she took daily, her pain was excruciating. Now, she was asking Dr. Dy to place just one needle in the site of her most intense pain. It was heartbreaking to watch. I tried to back her chair out of the room, but Dr. Dy put his hand up and waved me away, softly saying, "Leave us." I assumed that he was just planning to let Mom down gently while still "saving face" for her by sending me away so that he could explain to her in privacy that she was beyond help. I left the room and waited in the lobby, a bit perplexed by my strange determination to bring her down this futile road.

About 15 minutes later, Mrs. Dy approached me and said, "You've got to see this." I followed her down the hall and stopped as she motioned me into a treatment room on the left. Stepping into the room, I gasped aloud and jumped backwards into the hall. Mom was reclining in a large table/chair that looked almost like a birthing bed. Draped in a patient gown, her body was completely punctured with long, silver needles. Her legs, her arms, her torso, her neck, even her face, were covered with protruding, pulsating needles! Her glazed eyes glowered with the most peaceful expression I'd ever seen. Still, I almost fainted from the sight of all those needles. There had to be almost 100 of them! I rushed back to the waiting room, pacing back and forth as though I had just committed a terrible crime and needed to contemplate a quick getaway. That many needles would probably kill her! If I could get her out of this building alive, maybe I could take her back to the hospital. I paced like a crazy woman, sweating and muttering to myself that I was an idiot for thinking I could help her. Thank God no one else was in the room to witness my panic.

Fifteen or 20 minutes passed. Just as I was about to have a complete nervous breakdown, Mrs. Dy touched my arm and said, "Your Mama is ready to go home now." I quickly grabbed Mom's wheel-chair, which had been placed in the waiting room by the hall entrance, eager to load my obviously near-dead mother into it and get her the hell out of this whacked-out place. "Your Mama won't be needing that," Mrs. Dy said, smiling.

"Oh, you don't understand," I smirked, "She's been in this chair for over two years. She can't walk without it." I was trying to wrest the chair handles away from her.

Motioning with a nod toward the hall, Mrs. Dy said, "Look."

I turned toward the hall and witnessed a stark-staring miracle. My mother was walking/gliding toward me with her head held high and her entire body flowing with an ease and grace that defied the past 20 years of her life. She glided right up to me and said, in a clear and regal tone, "I'll be walking to the car, dear." Speechless, I rushed to open the door for her and followed closely behind her with the wheelchair, sure her legs would give out at any second. She glided all the way to the car.

On the ride home, Mom slowly and gracefully turned her head left and right as she viewed a world she hadn't seen for years. Arriving at her house, she walked the entire length of the front entrance and steadily climbed the porch steps to the front door. Although no one in our family had yet been told that I had flown in the day before and had gotten Mom released from the hospital that morning, her living room was filled with her children and their families, all waiting for her arrival as though they somehow knew everything that had just transpired. Mom spent the rest of the afternoon basking in her family's affection and her new-found freedom from pain and disfigurement.

Over the next seven weeks, Mom went to see Dr. Dy three times the first week, twice the second week and once a week thereafter. On the seventh week, when I found her in the kitchen at 7:00 in the morning washing dishes and dancing the hula, I knew it was time to go back to work. I called my boss and arranged to be transferred to a resort closer to home so that I could keep an eye on Mom. After a brief stay in Las Vegas to earn my real estate license for Nevada, I was transferred to a resort property in Reno. It was there that I met up with my "spice rack" blond angel again . . .

# My Angel

*Nothing could have prepared me for the moment I first met my Angel*
*It was eight feet tall, purest white, and was complete,*
*without gender*
*Its wings were as wide as its height, which was tricky to gage*
*As it floated in the air above me in the middle of the night*

*Only three feet of distance separated us as we faced each other*
*Building a bridge between Heaven and Earth*
*We embraced arms, and as we touched*
*I could only exclaim, "My Angel!"*
*All of my hopes, my distant memories of Reality*
*The forgotten Truth of who we are*
*Flooded through my heart*

*This was not just any ordinary Angel*
*I knew beyond a shadow of a doubt this was my Angel*
*Somehow, it was me!*
*Beckoned to my presence from the highest realm by request of my Spirit*
*A profound and loving statement from God—"Remember."*

# THE VISITORS

During my recent seven-week stay with Mom I had enrolled in a distance learning program to study metaphysics. The decision to enroll was not quite as dramatically inspired as had been my decision to study natural health, but this step felt essential at the time. As it turned out, the lessons from the new school proved instrumental in advancing my spiritual escapades to a whole new level. The course taught insights into self-awareness based on a yoga discipline. I had studied yoga postures for years as a young wife and mother. Now, I was being introduced to the philosophy of peace and prosperity through positive mental re-programming. Each lesson ended with a "prayer treatment" that was to be repeated before meditating.

Now living and working in Reno, Nevada, I had begun to devote a couple of hours a day to learning this meditation/prayer technique. One summer afternoon my son, Steven, who was attending university nearby, and a close friend, Emily, whose husband worked with me at the resort, and I went to see a movie. It was the most frightening movie I'd ever seen. Though it later earned a prestigious award, I can't begin to imagine how many viewers were emotionally scarred by the scenes in this film. I was horrified. Arriving home afterwards, I locked and bolted my door and sat in my living room, afraid of the entire world and everyone in it. My frequency was vibrating at such a low level, I could feel my interior trembling. I never wanted to leave the safety of my apartment again.

I was still sitting in my living room late that evening, trying to shake off the pervasive fear that had invaded my senses, when there was a knock at my door. It was about 11:00 p.m., way too late for visitors. I looked at my room-mate, who was snacking in the kitchen. For some unfathomable reason, I went to the door and opened it without even asking who was there or looking through the peep-hole. Suddenly, I felt no more fear. Two young adults, one a female and the other a male, were standing on my doorstep. They explained that they were with a sales crew from another country and that they were traveling around the U.S. on a bus selling laser-print art. Since my apartment was at the very end of the third floor of the last building in a large complex, I figured that it would be perfectly normal for them to be at my door so late in the evening, especially if they had already visited all of the other hundred-plus apartments. I ushered them into my living room, eager to see their laser-prints, which was highly unusual for me since I had virtually no cash to spend and I was sure they didn't take checks or credit cards. Still, I asked them to show me every print. The laser prints were all beautiful, but I immediately fell in love with one depicting a serene landscape of an ocean beach dotted with footprints in the sand. Superimposed over the scene was the verse, "Footprints," author unknown. In case you are one of the few people who hasn't heard this prayer, I'll repeat it here. Before that night, I had never heard of it myself . . .

*"One night a man had a dream. He dreamed he was walking along the beach with the Lord. Across the sky flashed scenes from his life. For each scene, he noticed two sets of footprints in the sand; one belonged to him and the other to the Lord. When the last scene of his life flashed before him, he looked back at the footprints in the sand. He noticed that many times along the path of his life there was only one set of footprints. He also noticed that it happened at the very lowest and saddest times in his life. This really bothered him and he questioned the Lord about it. 'Lord, You said that once I decided to follow You, You'd walk with me all the way. But I have noticed that during the most troublesome times in my life there is only one set of footprints. I don't understand why when I needed You the most You would leave me.' The Lord replied, 'My precious, precious child, I love you and I would never leave you. During your times of trial and suffering, when you see only one set of footprints, it was then that I carried you.'"*

Clutching the laser-print, I asked the young woman how much she wanted for it. "Fifteen dollars," she replied. Her voice had a European inflection and seemed to echo ever so slightly. I loved hearing it. The young man stood back and said nothing during the entire time they were there, which was only about 15 or 20 minutes. At no time did my room-mate, still munching in the kitchen, seem to notice that we had company, handing over the $15 I needed without a glance or a question. As I gave the young woman the money, she thanked me politely and bowed her head slightly as she and the young man left. For some reason, I didn't want them to go. I watched them walk away, noticing their dress and appearance. He was dark, with curly hair and a medium height and build. He was wearing long shorts, sneakers and a tee-shirt. She was very tall, with a perfect alabaster complexion, no make-up, and chin-length blond hair. She was wearing a yellow top, white shorts and white sneakers. I knew as they walked away that they had taken my fear away with them. I slept peacefully that night.

The next day I called my friend, Emily, who also lived in the apartment complex, to see which laser-print she had bought. She told me that she had been home all evening but had not received a visit from my young sales crew. Later that afternoon, when visiting the manager's office, I asked about the other tenants. Had they been visited by the laser-print sales crew? The manager called several friends who lived in different buildings of the same complex and none of them had seen my young visitors. Further checking revealed that no one in the complex had been visited that night by anyone selling laser-prints. I was baffled! Why did they tell me they were part of a sales crew that was sweeping throughout the apartment complex, selling laser-prints? And why show up so late at night? And how could they know that I was in desperate need of encouragement after seeing a movie that so horrified me that I was totally enveloped in fear? I'll tell you how . . .

I only realized who they were about five years later when I was living back home in California and taking care of my mother. I had met a young woman named Marlene who lived in a small Gold Rush town in the Sierra foothills called Knights Ferry. We became friends after my sister introduced us at a library meeting. One night, Marlene called me about midnight, surprised and exhilarated at the same time. She had been depressed all afternoon and evening, realizing despondently that she didn't even have a picture of Jesus in her house so that she could look at him as she prayed for healing from her deep depression. Suddenly, at 11:00 p.m., there was a knock at her door. Marlene's house sat at the top of a very high hill, with about 15 houses situated alongside the steep road leading up to it. Anyone coming to her house would have had to approach from that road. When Marlene heard the knock, she looked out of her window at her driveway. There were no other vehicles besides hers. Whoever was at her door must have walked up that hill to her house. Two young people, a male and a female, were standing on her porch, holding a stack of artwork. As Marlene opened the door, the couple explained that they were selling laser-prints to the residents of the town and that her house was their last stop. You guessed it. They had a beautiful laser-print picture of Jesus and it cost only $15! I asked Marlene to describe the couple. She perfectly described my visitors of five years earlier, down to their complexions, hair, accent, and even the color of their tee-shirts and shorts. Of course, after checking with her neighbors the next day she discovered that no one else on her street had been visited by them that night, either. By now, we were sure they were angels, bringing us what we needed most at that moment to restore our faith—mine in the world and its people, and Marlene's in herself. Both times, the message was Christ.

# In Your Eyes

*Did you know that every time I look into your eyes*
*I see God*
*Back there, in the corner*
*Winking at me in a come-hither kind of way*
*This is why people have often told you*
*That they feel like they're falling into your eyes*
*Dark pools of memory, knocking us slightly off kilter*

*I believe this is where Santa got his twinkle*
*The generosity of God dancing in his eyes*
*And his mirth is shown through many eyes*
*Just before it lands in your belly*

*His profound loyalty gazes at us*
*Through the eyes of our pets*
*Which also carry the key to a secret passageway*
*They will someday lead us through*

*But love, ah God's love is in every eye, of every person*
*Every animal, every creature and form of life,*
*Known and yet to be*
*Whether the window we view it through*
*Is opened or closed*

# MOVING ON

During the 18 months I lived and worked in Reno, I also ran a small wellness center in an acupressure school downtown. Once again, I was purchasing Nutripathic Formulas in bulk for my weight-loss clients. In the meantime, I visited Mom every week or two. She lived about three hours from me, so the trip was usually a weekend turnaround, which also gave me a chance to visit my daughter and grandson, who lived a few miles from Mom, and my sisters and brothers, who all lived a short distance from her as well. Often, my family and friends from home would come up to Reno to visit me for a few days. With the night-life there, we always had a great time. Because I worked for a resort company, I could occasionally get tickets to shows and events. When the call came transferring me to another resort property back East, I felt a little sad, knowing that I would miss my family and our fun in the "Biggest Little City in the World."

Before leaving, I made sure Mom was regularly seeing Dr. Dy and following the holistic protocol I had placed her on. She was doing so well those days that she and my step-dad had purchased a boat and a motor-home and had enrolled with a local RV camping vacation program. They spent almost every weekend at the vacation property, fishing and enjoying the great outdoors. It was as though someone had turned back the hands of time for Mom. She responded so well to the acupuncture/vitamin regimen that I thought she would live forever. What I didn't realize was that my frequent visits home on weekends had been the catalyst she needed to stay the course.

As soon as I began my cross-country road-trip to Virginia, where I had been assigned to work, Mom visited her local medical clinic and asked if they had a Chinese doctor who might administer acupuncture to her and bill her insurance for it. Dr. Dy's office didn't accept her insurance, so Mom had been paying out-of-pocket for her monthly acupuncture treatments. On a fixed income, she wanted to save the monthly expense and figured that any Chinese doctor would be trained in Chinese medicine as well as allopathic medicine. God bless her heart. She tried to call me first to get my opinion, but I was driving with my room-mate on a six-day trek across the continent. There were no cell phones in those days, so I was unreachable. Had I known what was about to happen, I would never have left.

The Chinese doctor the medical clinic's receptionist sent Mom to see was a heart specialist. He determined that she had congestive heart failure and scheduled her for bypass surgery. By the time I heard the news, it was too late. I flew out and rushed to her side. This time though, she didn't rally when I entered the room. Unconscious, she was whiter than ever before. As I stood next to her, I felt her die. There was a sudden rush of *death* that flashed through my body. I will never forget how that felt. Everything in her existence just came to a screeching halt and then quickly poured out through my feet and entered the earth below. I turned white and almost fainted on the spot. About two hours later, Mom finally regained consciousness. Yes, she was still alive, but the quality of her life was forever gone. From that moment, she never walked under her own steam again—that is until four months before her death.

I stayed until Mom was sent home from the hospital. Bedridden, she began to develop blood clots and had to be put on blood-thinners. Now, she was no longer a candidate for acupuncture, as it required needles, which could be dangerous for a patient on blood-thinners. Nor could I continue her protocol of vitamins and herbs, as any nutrient with vitamin K could adversely affect her blood's viscosity while interacting with the blood-thinners. Now, the remainder of Mom's life would be spent in a bed and a wheelchair. I was heartbroken.

Over the next eight years, Mom would develop diabetes, stroke, the return of her rheumatoid arthritis and its crippling pain, and, finally, cancer. As the anti-inflammatory steroids were used in ever-increasing amounts for her pain, she lost immune function and began to develop pneumonia repeatedly throughout the years. It was a critical case of pneumonia in 1994 that caused her, once again hospitalized, to call me and beg me to come home for the last time. Her doctors explained that she might only live another six or seven months. She couldn't survive another episode of pneumonia. This was her eighth bout in two years.

On the spur of the moment, I agreed. Something in her voice made me decide that this time I needed to take a long leave of absence from my job and spend the last months of Mom's life with her. I didn't think I had any more tricks in my little black bag that could reverse her misery and prolong her life. But that was before I knew just how powerfully the human body can respond to love, nature and energy-work. I was yet to learn the techniques of Reiki, but the groundwork was being laid. Between Mom's quadruple bypass surgery in 1991 and the phone call from her asking me to come home in 1994, I experienced a plethora of spiritual awakenings that were necessary to prepare me for the work that was still ahead of me, first with Mom and then with hundreds, perhaps thousands of students, teachers and readers. I would begin to learn the techniques, principles and disciplines that would help me fulfill my divine purpose on this earth—*to assist you in the restoration of your memory of being Home with God . . .*

# *When Your Spirit Dances*

*You are exquisitely beautiful*
*When your Spirit dances*
*Which is almost always, all days*
*You have no idea how celebrated you are*
*Even in your darkest hours, your spirit dances*

*Your sway may be slowed with melancholy*
*Sending signals, asking for a hug or two*
*A warm embrace to stir your soul*
*And rekindle a flame of passion*
*That may express itself in a tango for two*
*Or a waltz of elegance*
*To restore your vision of beauty*

*Sometimes your spirit dances solo*
*Opening the stage with swirling colors of creation*
*As you twist and turn to the vibrant music*
*Of enthusiasm*
*While reminiscing about the good old days*
*Of a tap on every toe*

*Revel in the dance of dreams, dear one*
*As you remember your steps*
*The ebb and flow of life*
*When your spirit dances*

# TRAVELS WITHIN

It was the fall of 1991. I had been living and working in Colonial Williamsburg, Virginia, for less than a month when I had my first bona-fide, fully conscious, fully awake *Out-Of-Body* travel experience. I had been practicing the meditation/prayer treatments from the texts of the metaphysical lessons for about a year when I realized that I needed to stop working for the resort for a while and dedicate myself to my spiritual studies. One night as I was preparing for bed, I read through the entire 48 post-chapter prayer treatments of my metaphysical texts, which took about 45 minutes to an hour to read. Finishing the prayers, I laid across my bed with my arms and legs positioned like DaVinci's "Vitruvian Man" drawing. I then began a series of *chakra expansions*, beginning with the crown chakra and moving down through the six remaining chakras slowly and intentionally. I had no idea why I was doing this very unusual exercise. Normally, chakra clearings are begun at the root, or base, chakra and then carried consecutively upward to the crown. Instead, I was expanding my chakras in reverse.

Chakras are spinning wheels of rainbow-colored energy, invisible to the naked eye, that are aligned with the body's Vega nerve and endocrine system and situated above and along the spinal column from the top of the head to the base of the spine. The crown chakra is considered our spiritual energy entrance point, through which we access our highest spiritual awareness and connection to *Home with God*. Through this chakra, we also extend a silver cord, or lifeline, that tethers us to our physical body when we travel to other dimensions or planes of existence. The crown chakra is violet in color.

The next chakra is situated in the center of the forehead, just above the eyebrows and is the color indigo (deep blue/purple.) This chakra activates our "second sight," which enables us to *see* with our eyes closed while in meditation or prayer. There is a yoga technique that enables us to activate our ability to see with our second sight which I'll describe here:

> Light a candle and stare into it for two to three minutes. There will be an imprint left on your inner screen when you close your eyes, much like the image left when a camera flashes in your eyes. Blow out the candle (so you don't burn down the house while seeking enlightenment) and lie down comfortably on your back.
>
> Look into the space approximately six inches in front of your face, where the candle light has imprinted your inner screen. Now, elevate your inner gaze about an inch or two, so that your eyes are shifted slightly upwards. Peer into this inner field of energy and you'll begin to notice colors and, possibly, cloudlike formations. As the clouds part, peer through the opening. You are now looking into a realm of higher frequency, one that is around you but is also within you.

As you practice this exercise, you'll experience more visions and spiritual awakenings. Eventually, you'll travel into this field of energy through a tunnel or tube of light and experience other dimensions of reality. Ultimately, you'll travel past all of the myriad alternate realms, cross the border between the *dream of living* and the *Reality of Life*, and find yourself, just for a moment or two, fully awake and conscious *within the presence of your Creator in the only True residence you've ever known—Home with God*. In that moment, you will realize that *you have never left this place of Life. You've been Here, Home with God, all along*, while you were experiencing your current dream of living as though it were the only true reality and as if God were somehow separate from you. It's really all a matter of perception. Our lens has been skewed for a very long time. With intention, we can adjust our lens back into focus and end the feelings of abandonment and fear that permeate our (dream) world and align ourselves once again with our *Greater Reality—that we have always been, are now, and always will be Home with God* . . .

Our true nature embodies unconditional love, compassion and forgiveness—the attributes given to us by our Father/Mother God. *This is what is real.* Everything else, including all emotions and feelings based on fear, are born from the false belief that we are somehow separate from God. Once we realize that no separation ever took place, except in our erroneous thoughts, we reaffirm our rightful inheritance of honor, tolerance, and dignity and begin to view our lives as an adventure rather than as a challenge. *More than this, I cannot ask.* In order for us to remember this profound knowledge, we need to *have faith as a mustard seed* or, lacking that, find the opportunity to experience ourselves restored, for just an instant, to our one true residence—*Home with God.* Now that's an *aha* moment that can change your life! Before you try the chakra expansion exercise and begin traipsing around the inner universe, however, you need to read the rest of this chapter (and maybe a few others.) So, let's get on with it . . .

The next chakra is the throat chakra, located just above the collar bone. This chakra is blue and is utilized in speaking your voice, both externally and internally. Deception adversely affects this chakra. We should always strive to speak our truth, given that our truth is based on love rather than fear. In the Frequency Elevator chapter, I'll introduce EFT—Emotional Freedom Technique—which can dramatically shift your feelings and emotions out of a fear gear and into a much higher expression of feelings and speech, one in which you'll have a much easier time speaking your personal truth with love and dignity.

The next chakra is in your heart and its color is green. Sometimes people who are deeply in love can see the heart chakra's resplendent emerald green radiance between them when they embrace. All of your other chakras receive balancing and healing when you breathe in light through your heart chakra. The technique is simple. Touch your thumb to your index finger lightly as you breathe in through your nose to the count of four while focusing on your heart chakra and state silently, "*I breathe in light through the center of my heart.*" On the exhale, breathing out through your lips, focus on the area just below your navel. It's called the "Ha" center. Counting again to four, direct the healing energy you have just breathed in through your heart chakra toward this Ha center, saying silently, "*Take this vital source and store it.*" Repeat this process, touching your thumb to the next finger with each breath, as many times as you feel is appropriate for your body. Go through each of your four fingers for up to ten breaths each, if needed. This exercise actually recharges the batteries in your cells. You'll feel energized and revitalized when you're done. I always end this and any other prayer, meditation or exercise with, "*Thank You, God.*"

Just below your heart chakra is your solar plexus chakra, midway between your heart and your navel. The solar plexus chakra is yellow in color and relates to our emotional connections to our families and friends. When we fear losing someone dear to us, we often feel a constriction in our solar plexus chakra, usually manifesting in the form of nausea or a "sinking" feeling in the pit of our stomach. When someone is fearful of loss, he is often called "yellow," as though being perceived as a coward. Our chakra colors are actually visible to some people, which explains the common practice of using color to describe a feeling. "Blue" often describes sadness that may be unexpressed through words, so the blue throat chakra may be flashing its feelings. "Green" with envy may depict unrequited love felt by the heart.

At the navel, we express our creativity through the orange chakra. Vibrancy, vitality, vivaciousness, exuberance, etc., are all expressed by the orange hue of the navel chakra. Isn't it interesting that we call oranges "navel oranges?"

Lastly, our root chakra, located at the pelvis, is red. Our root chakra reflects our passions, (don't we women all have a red dress?) our anger, (seeing red) and our dangers, (stop sign, red flag) as well as our debts, (in the red). Our root chakra is also our grounding anchor, keeping us "rooted" in practicality.

These seven colors are also the seven color-rays of the rainbow. They reflect the three primary colors—red, yellow and blue, with the overlapping hues of green (blue combined with yellow,) orange (red combined with yellow,) and violet/indigo (blue combined with red). As beautiful as these seven colors are when reflected through light and water, they comprise only a slender segment of the vast spectrum of color in existence. However, from our common perspective, which I and many others call 3-D (third dimensional), it has been shown that focusing on the seven rainbow chakra colors will increase our vibratory frequency and enhance our spiritual awareness, enabling us to experience dimensions beyond our typical perception.

On some level, our experiences are always the result of our intentions, whether we realize it at the time or not. An enormous focus of intense and widespread study has been circulating for years that is allowing mainstream society to recognize the potential of giving more *attention* to our *intentions*. Books such as "The Power of Intention," by Dr. Wayne Dyer; "Ask and it is Given," by Esther and Jerry Hicks; "The New Earth," by Eckhart Tolle; and "Adventures in Manifesting" by Sean Patrick and Sarah Prout all are current bestsellers designed to acquaint their readers with the empowering message of self-actualization through the *action* of intentional thought. Decades ago, this message was also introduced by "The Power of Positive Thinking," by Dr. Norman Vincent Peale; "The Greatest Salesman in the World," by Og Mandino; "The Power of Belief," by Claude Bristol; and "Think and Grow Rich," by Napoleon Hill; to name just a few. The authors of these works, and many others, are bringing the message of self-empowerment to a world that often feels disempowered and disenchanted.

Blame, guilt, greed, judgment, helplessness and victimization are served up to the masses daily through television entertainment and news stories. As we refuse to consume the negative messages being sold to us through adverse sensationalism and instead favor uplifting, empowering and inspiring stories and reading material, we can shift the focus in our lives from destruction and despair to hope, compassion and healing. This shift enables us to consider the possibility that we can experience forgiveness as a feeling or action of *empowering intention*, rather than as an unlikely gift of acquiescence that is often withheld, even for a lifetime, as a means of punishment or falsely perceived power.

Once we see the true power of forgiveness, we release ourselves from the bondage of blame and begin to truly heal. As this happens, our twisted and constricted chakras begin to spin in harmonious beauty and balance, propelling our perceptions beyond the dream of fear and lack into the multi-dimensional *house of many mansions* that exists in our higher realms of perception. Having witnessed these realms, we are then able to travel higher and higher until we awaken *Home With God* and realize that we have been *There (Here)* all along. If you feel ready to travel this road now, I cannot think of a better time to embark on your journey. So grab a candle, close the door, dim the lights and let's *go within* . . .

# THE CHAKRA MEDITATION

Be sure the temperature in your room is comfortable. Have a light blanket handy. After gazing into a candle flame for a few minutes, blow out the candle and lie down on your back with your arms and legs uncrossed. Gaze upward, eyes closed, into the imprinted light image from the candle flame. As the light image fades, begin with a silent prayer from your heart. (You will know instinctively what to say.) Or you may choose to silently repeat a simple statement such as, *"I knock on the door to the kingdom of Heaven. Let it open to me now,"* or *"Peace, be still, and know that I am Home With God now and forever."* One or both of these statements can be repeated as many times as you feel is appropriate for you. There is no need to count. This is an intensely personal experience and you will know instinctively from within your own spiritual awareness how far you should go. (At some point during this exercise, you may feel a vibration occurring in your body. This is normal and indicates an elevation in your frequency.)

Begin to expand your chakras by envisioning the color violet emanating from your crown chakra. If you don't *see* the color, just imagine that it's there. As you do, also imagine that the violet color is now very slowly enveloping your entire body, inside and out, and expanding outward from you until it fills the room with its violet radiance. Now envision that the violet radiance is expanding into the entire house or apartment, filling it with radiant violet color. Allow the violet radiance to expand until it fills the city around your home. As it expands further, slowly allow the violet color to envelope the entire country and then, finally, the world. Imagine the entire planet glowing with violet radiance, shimmering and bathed, with all of her inhabitants, in your healing violet light. Hold this image for a few seconds.

Now, bringing your attention back to yourself, envision an indigo or purple/blue ball of light centered in your forehead. Again, very slowly allow this ball of indigo light to fill your body, then let it flow outward from you into the room, then outward from your room to your home, flowing further from your home throughout your city and then your country until, lastly, you surround the earth in brilliant indigo light, overlapping the still-violet earth with indigo brilliance. Now you have enveloped the earth in a layer of violet light and a layer of indigo light. Hold this image for a few seconds.

Returning your focus to yourself, envision a brilliant ball of blue light emanating from your throat. As before, very slowly allow this blue light to fill your body, then the room, then your city and country until, lastly, you surround the still-indigo earth with your brilliant blue light. Now the earth is shimmering with a layer of violet, which is covered with a layer of indigo, which is now covered with a layer of blue. Again, hold this image for a few seconds.

Bringing your awareness back to your body, envision a green ball of light radiating from your heart. Very slowly, expand this green light until it fills your body, then the room, then your city, your country and, lastly, the earth, in its green radiance. Now the earth is layered with the shimmering colors of violet, indigo, blue and green. Hold this image for a few seconds.

As you return your focus to your body once again, notice a brilliant yellow ball of light radiating from your solar plexus area, midway between your heart and your navel. Very slowly, expand this yellow light into and around your body, your room, your city, your country and, finally, the earth, with the brilliant yellow light now overlapping the green light, which overlaps the blue light, which overlaps the indigo light, which overlaps the violet light. Hold this image for a few seconds.

Coming back to yourself, now envision a vibrant orange ball of light emanating from your navel area. Very slowly, allow this brilliant orange color to fill your body, then your room, your city, your country and, lastly, the earth, which is now shimmering in your orange light as it covers the yellow light, which covers the green light, which covers the blue light, which covers the indigo light, which covers the violet light. Hold this image for a few seconds.

Finally, returning once again to yourself, envision a brilliant ball of red light emanating from your root chakra, or pelvis region, and begin very slowly to fill your body with it, slowly expanding the red light from your body outward to fill your room, then your city, then your country and, lastly, the earth, wrapping the red light's brilliance around the orange light. Now the earth is layered in violet, indigo, blue, green, yellow, orange and red, all shimmering in rainbow brilliance. Hold this image for a few seconds or until your focus shifts elsewhere.

You may be experiencing an expanded state of awareness. Whatever you feel or experience now is appropriate for you at this time. Go with it. Allow yourself the gift of higher perception. You may just fall into a deep sleep. If you do, images in your dreams may be messages to your conscious mind from your higher self, or Spirit. Let your mind relax and follow your intuitive nature. Be curious. You won't hurt yourself unless you're a sleepwalker and you fall off the bed, and if that's the case, you should have someone observe you while you meditate.

The first time I did this exercise, I thought I was experiencing an earthquake. My frequency shifted to such a high calibration that I virtually blasted into a brilliant blue sky on the inner planes and traveled a great distance, observing several golden symbols and shapes as I flew through them. First, there was a golden circle, then a square, then a triangle and, last, a music note. Realizing that I had traveled a seemingly great distance, I thought, "*I wonder if I can get back?*" Instantly, I returned to my body and the experience was over. In her bestselling book, *Out on a Limb*, and the subsequent movie of the same name, Shirley MacLaine describes an out-of-body experience she had while meditating in a hot-spring natural pool in Peru with her friend and guide, David. In Shirley's experience, she saw the silver cord that connected her higher self to her physical body. I didn't see the silver cord on my first OBE; however I have seen it on later journeys. You may or may not see your silver cord during your travels, but just know that it's there in any case. It keeps you connected to your physical body so you can never get lost.

Each time you repeat this chakra exercise, you'll increase your frequency until it is re-calibrated to the level you seek. Eventually, using this exercise and a variety of other methods we'll cover in later chapters, you'll reach the frequency of *Home With God*. After that happens, I fully expect to be reading about your experiences in *your* book!

## *You Are the Chosen One*

*Out of a clear blue sky*
*On a still and quiet afternoon*
*A very familiar voice will speak*
*Softly into your ear*
*"You are the chosen one"*
*There will be absolutely no question*
*Whatsoever in your mind*
*That you have just experienced reality*
*And that a pivotal moment in your life*
*Has occurred*

*You may look around the room*
*Seeking the one*
*For whom you have been entrusted*
*To deliver this exquisite message*
*Only to find out that you are alone*
*Or at least you thought you were*

*For a while, you'll live in the dream*
*Of denial*
*Fully expecting the world to prove*
*Your conviction*
*That you are unworthy*
*And could never be considered*
*A chosen one*
*By anyone*
*Least of all the voice for God*

*So you'll ask yourself*
*What am I supposed to do with this?*
*Does this mean I'm different?*
*Until you realize your need to deny*
*And declare doubt of your worth*
*Are only garments of your ego*
*The main blockage to remembrance*
*That we are all one*
*The chosen one*

# HIATUS

Shortly after my chakra clearing adventure, I experienced two additional memorable events of a spiritual nature while living in Virginia. The first event led to the writing and eventual publishing of my first book, *FigureShaping*. The second event led to a visit *Home With God* on a mountaintop in New Hampshire and will hopefully culminate, in the not too distant future, with a visit to the Grand Teton Mountain Range of Wyoming.

One fall morning, while gazing at the misty Williamsburg countryside from my living room window, having just resigned from my position at the resort property, I wondered pensively how I would now fill my days. Of course, spiritual studies were my prime reason for taking this hiatus from work, but I knew there would still be enough time left over each day for some additional pursuit of accomplishment. (Sorry. I'm an Aries.) While mentally drifting through these thoughts and, at the same time, admiring the mystical view of the morning autumn scene outside my window, I heard His voice speak aloud to me for the fourth time in my life, *"Write your book."*

"What book?" I feigned innocence. This was a little more than I felt ready for.

*"You know what book."*

Oops. I almost forgot. Nothing, not a miniscule speck of *anything* can be pulled over on Him. Time to fess up. Time to write a book! But what book? Obviously, the book you're now reading needed 20 more years of spiritual experiences for material before it could be written.

So the only book left would be one that embraced my other lifelong passion—natural health and weight-loss. I scrambled to the kitchen/ dining room and rummaged through a box of work supplies from my office that was still sitting on top of the dining room table. There was a stack of yellow legal pads and a box of pens. There you go, girl! All conditions have been met. The history has been lived. The workplace has been put on hold. The tools are ready. The assignment has been issued. So now, let's write a book!

My routine was simple. For three months, I followed a strict regimen. Up at 7:00 a.m. Oatmeal for breakfast. Ballet stretches and exercises for 20 minutes. Quick pick-up around the house. Pen in hand at 10:00 sharp. *Listen and allow. Write the words as they come.* Put down the pen at 7:00 p.m. The phone didn't ring during the hours I was writing. No one came to my door. I barely noticed my room-mate's comings and goings. I was on a mission and I carried it to completion without interruption.

By the end of three months, the book was half done. I returned to work, writing in the staff lounge between settlements. (I was a loan officer.) Within another three months, the book was finished. I put it away until a local newspaper publisher asked to print it in installments in his weekly newspaper. After that, the book was relegated to a "stuff" box for another few years until it was finally converted, in 1998, to a typed format on my first computer and introduced as a class text for the just-founded school I had inherited from Dr. Martin, the Holistic Life Institute. Finally, in 2007, I heard the words, *"Publish your book."* It had been almost 17 years since I had written the book I was now being asked to publish.

"What book?" I had to try.

*"You know what book."*

And so it happened that after so many years I finally sent *FigureShaping* to a publisher. The first publishing house I sent it to picked it up immediately. (I had been directed to them in a dream.) This book you are now reading, even while still in the writing phase, was picked up by still another publisher that I was directed (by Him) to contact shortly after hearing those simple words again in the summer of 2008, "*Write your book.*"

Dare I say again, "What book?" I don't think so! So here we are, you and I, sharing these simple stories for reasons only He knows. Someday, we'll sit back and sip a margarita while reminiscing about the trials and tribulations we encountered while seeking a place that was right in front of our very eyes all along—*Home With God* . . .

At the beginning of this segment, I stated that two events of a spiritual nature occurred while I was living in Virginia. With the writing of *FigureShaping* being the first event, I'll now describe the second. It was a vision. Fully awake, fully conscious, and quite startling. And, again, more real than reality. I had just climbed into bed and closed my eyes one night in January, 1992, when I noticed a pin-point of light on my inner screen. Suddenly, the light began to expand into a circle, and then a rectangle, until it was about the size of a small screen (like a viewfinder) in front of my eyes. Through this "viewfinder," I could see with crystal clarity a mountain range fronted by a huge meadow. The mountain range was beautiful but totally unfamiliar to me. As I stared into the scene, I heard the words, "*You're going to the Tetons.*"

Until then, I had never heard of a "Teton." Turns out they're a magnificent range of mountains in Wyoming. The next morning, I looked up the Teton Mountains in a travel magazine from work. The article depicted a two-page spread that was exactly identical to the scene I had witnessed in my vision. Although I still have not visited the Teton Mountains, I fully expect that within the next few years I will find myself there in yet another spiritual event. Until then, I have a few extraordinary moments on another mountaintop to share with you. The next stop in my spiritual saga takes us to New Hampshire and to an event that was witnessed by hundreds and was even reported on the front page of the local newspaper! The light of *Home with God* blazed right through the veils of darkness and cascaded its brilliance upon a mountaintop in New Hampshire. I witnessed the event firsthand because, well, I happened to be sleeping on that very mountaintop when it occurred!

It was the summer of '93. I had been living and working in New Hampshire near Lake Winnipesauke for several months after transferring there from Virginia. In mid–August, I went on an overnight hiking trip with a mountain trail guide. We hiked to the top of Mount Webster in the Presidential Range of the White Mountains. Reaching the summit at night-fall, we had to use flashlights to set up camp and cook dinner. By 9:00 p.m., I was exhausted and ready to turn in for the night. My guide noticed some strange lights in the sky overhead and suggested that I stay up a little longer to watch them with him. Over the next 30 minutes, we watched the sky literally open like a stage curtain as light from the "other side of the sky" rained down on the vast heavens. There were two openings in the sky that night, crossing each other in the center and reaching all the way to the horizon on either side. It was as though the sky had been divided into four equal sections by light pouring in from *somewhere beyond* the sky. I asked if the curtain of light could be the "northern lights" (the Aurora Borealis) that I had always heard so much about. My guide explained that he had been a mountain trail guide for over 30 years and had never seen anything like this! Then I suggested that the lights must be a reflection from a nearby city. Negative. The nearest town was over 30 miles away. Besides, the nearest city wasn't *on the other side of the sky!*

Quite astounded by the vast shower of lights, my guide decided to stay up and watch for as long as it persisted. I was unable to stay awake and reluctantly turned in, falling into a deep sleep as soon as my head hit the pillow. Suddenly, about an hour later, I awoke to a brilliant light within, accompanied by an ecstatic celebration, even more intense than the inner light experience in Florida had been! I felt that I was being *welcomed home.* Within minutes, I sank back into deep sleep, reminding myself that I needed to tell my guide about it in the morning. When I climbed out of my tent the next morning, he was already up brewing coffee. I hesitated to say anything at first, but then I just blurted out the whole thing, hoping he wouldn't think I was a nut. A look of relief flooded his face as he told me that he hadn't even been to bed! He had been up all night, walking all over the mountaintop in a brilliant light that was even brighter than the mid-day sunlight! He'd found trails that he'd never seen before and could even see the tiniest insects crawling in the earth. We were both flabbergasted.

Returning to the valley that afternoon, I picked up a local newspaper. There, on the front page, was our mysterious canopy of light, bathing Mount Webster in a brilliant glow! Someone had photographed the mountain from a distance. My guide and I were the only hikers on the mountain's summit that night. To this day, I still don't know what to make of that event. I can only surmise that *Home with God* broke through the veil to pay us a visit on *this* side!

# Everyday

*Everyday is a lesson, teaching me to trust*
*That tonight the sun will set*
*And rise again tomorrow*

*Everyday is a symbol that all is well*
*Even though my feelings*
*Often beg to differ*

*Everyday reminds me that this, too, will pass*
*The transition between having*
*And losing*

*The breech, the unsettled feeling*
*While waiting for Familiar to arrive*
*Yet longing for what was*
*And praying for what might be*

*Everyday will continue to pass*
*In its own way*
*Asking me to trust in the miracle*
*That is everyday*

# COMING HOME

Eleven years had passed since my first move to the East Coast. For most of those years, I had worked for a resort development that frequently required moving to newly acquired properties. While in New Hampshire, I decided to leave the company and work for a local real estate firm. My son, Steven, had joined me after my move to the region and was enrolled in a local state university. His brother, Michael, was a practicing chiropractor in New Jersey. My daughter, Laura, was raising her family back home in California. Mom, hospitalized again, was battling with her eighth round of pneumonia in two years. Realizing that her days were numbered when she called me from the hospital pleading with me to come home, I took a leave of absence and flew to California. It was to be a seven-month visit, as Mom's doctors estimated that she had only that much longer to live. Arriving at the San Francisco airport, I was greeted by my sister, Darleen, with a hug and the directive, "You're going to learn Reiki!" Without a word, I agreed, nodding my head. It was time.

Mom was wearing an oxygen tube most of the time. She could walk from her bedroom to the couch, but had to lie down for the better part of her day. Still on blood thinners, she was unable to follow my vitamin/herb protocol, but Reiki seemed to be a huge boost to her health and vitality. Every day, she and my step-father sat in chairs in the dining room and quietly received the Reiki "attunements" from me. In spite of numerous continuing maladies and surgeries, Mom lived another five years. I realized within a few months of arriving in California that I wouldn't be returning to the East Coast. My son, Steven, also transferred to a local college and moved home.

From the moment I arrived back in California in March of 1994, my life has been under what I call *"divine ordinance."* When I said "yes" to learning Reiki, I actually said "yes" to fulfilling my divine purpose on earth. Little did I know at that time, however, just how monumental that purpose would be! Folks ask me occasionally what inspired me to open a school of massage therapy and holistic health in the small town where I was born after spending over a decade traveling the country and working and living in luxury resort areas. Did I just wake up one morning and say to myself, "I think I'll open a post-secondary school and spend the rest of my life training students in mind/body/spirit wellness?" Um . . . not quite! My plan was simple. Now that Mom was responding so well to Reiki and would probably live much longer that predicted, I decided to complement her Reiki healing with acupuncture, the sure-fire way to relieve her rheumatoid arthritis pain. The only obstacle to this was her medication. Because of the blood thinners, Mom was not eligible for acupuncture treatments by a licensed acupuncturist. Besides, her insurance wouldn't cover the treatments even if she had found an acupuncturist willing to treat her. The only solution was for me to become an acupuncturist and treat my mom myself! This way, I could open a small office and treat other local patients and offer them Reiki as well as acupuncture for their pain. Being her daughter, I had no fear of any adverse effects from utilizing the acupuncture needles with Mom's medication. I lived with her and could monitor her reactions closely. The plan sounded perfect.

My Reiki training took about four months. I was trained, along with three others, by two very spiritual Reiki Masters—Jeanette Woods and Gale Mellow. They had trained under William Rand, the Reiki Master who founded the International Center for Reiki Training in Springfield, Michigan. William also wrote the world's foremost Reiki training manual, *Reiki, the Healing Touch: First and Second Degree Manual,* through Vision Publications, which I require for all Reiki classes at my school and which I also highly recommend for anyone on the spiritual path. I had just completed my 2ⁿᵈ Degree Reiki training when I was given a very special Reiki "gift."

It was a hot, summer day. I was babysitting for my four-month-old nephew at Mom's house. Another older nephew was also visiting. Mom and my older nephew were napping in the living room. The air conditioner was humming. All of the heavy drapes were closed to the mid-day sun. I was quietly playing with the baby in his bouncy chair on the kitchen floor when, for no discernible reason, I stood up and stepped the few feet into the dark living room. There was a feeling of something major pending in the atmosphere of the room. Suddenly, I heard a voice speak out-loud next to me, "*Jan, get your camera and take a picture.*" It was the voice of my Reiki "guide," Tara, whom I had "met" in a vision during a meditation in my Second Degree Reiki class a few days before.

On this particular day, I had been staying with Mom and my step-dad for less than four months, living in the large "Florida room" at the rear of the house. Thinking I was only going to stay for seven months, I had packed and brought 17 boxes of clothing, grooming items, and essentials. My camera was undoubtedly at the very bottom of one of those boxes. It probably was unloaded, as I couldn't remember having used it for quite a while. I envisioned myself climbing into those heavy boxes desperately looking for a camera that didn't even have film in it, and probably breaking a fingernail in the process. This was not a good thing. I had a very powerful feeling that God was about to blast me with something that I would be able to document with photography and it probably couldn't wait until I found my stupid camera! Whatever was happening that I needed to photograph was happening now! I was sure to disappoint God and lose out on something big. Thinking the situation was hopeless, I folded my arms like a petulant child and said to myself, "Anyway, I didn't really hear a voice!"

"*Jan, just get your camera.*" This was as clear as day. I *had* heard Tara's voice! Whirling around ready to run to my room and slam through every box, if necessary, I stopped, mid-stride, and found myself staring at my camera. It was right in front of me, sitting on the counter between the kitchen and the living room! I didn't take the time to look and see if it was loaded. I turned it sideways and snapped a shot of my nephew, who was sleeping peacefully on a fold-out foam chair. As the shutter opened, I saw a large beam of light, about ten feet long and eight inches deep, emerge from the upper right corner of the room where the wall met the ceiling. In slow motion, it headed straight for me and turned at a ninety-degree angle directly in front of me, entering the camera and then plowing straight into my chest, lifting me a few inches off the floor!

As it entered my body, the beam of light exploded into brilliant fireworks that sparkled throughout the room for several seconds before fading away. The entire experience was accompanied by a feeling of an ocean wave crashing to shore and then returning to the sea. Steadying myself, I jumped back and took another picture, this time of the baby in the kitchen. I had a feeling that the "energy" was still there to a lesser degree as it was retreating. In the ensuing stillness, I calmly placed the camera back on the counter and said to myself, "None of this happened." I couldn't wrap my head around what I had just witnessed and experienced. I was never going to touch that camera again! I picked up the baby and went to my room. There, we slept for the rest of the afternoon, with Reiki "chills" streaming up and down my body the entire time. I was not going to mention this day to anyone, ever.

A few days later, my sister, Darleen, called me and told me to get out all of my photo film so that we could take it to a pharmacy to be developed. In our entire lives, at no time had my sister ever asked me to participate in film-developing with her! I told her that I didn't have any film to develop.

"Yes, you do," she countered. Within minutes, she showed up at the house, took me outside and insisted that I finish the roll in my camera by taking photos of the back yard (which was mostly weeds), and then she drove us to the pharmacy that offered the highest quality of printing. I went along with her, never expecting there to be anything of an ethereal nature on my 35 millimeter camera film exposures. In fact, I decided that I wouldn't even pick up the photos when they were processed. Why pay for pictures of an overgrown back yard?

Four days later, my sister showed up once again at the house and hustled me into her car so that we could drive to the pharmacy and get our prints. Walking through the store, I felt an angel at my shoulder, whispering to me, "Wait until you see those pictures!" Still, when we got to the photo counter, I didn't bother to open the envelope. Darleen enthusiastically tore into her packages of prints, thumbing through them right there. "What are you doing?" I asked her. I wasn't planning to look at my prints until I got home.

"I'm checking to see if they are all good. I don't want to pay for misprints," she explained. Thinking I wouldn't have to pay for *any* of my prints because they would all be worthless, I opened the envelope. On the top of the stack was the photo I had snapped of the large beam of light! I had caught it on film just before it bent toward the camera! I called the film processing manager over to look at the photo, asking him if the light beam could be explained by a defect in the camera or the film.

"I processed that picture myself and I was wondering the same thing," he said. "But no, it's not a defect. That's a photo of an actual light source." *No kidding*, I thought.

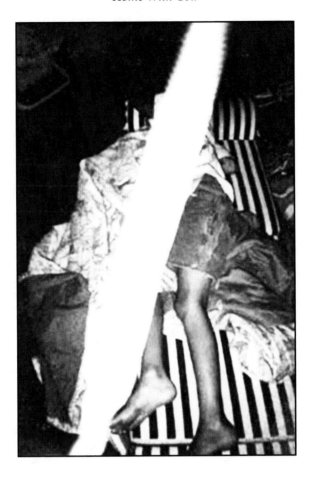

The second photo was of the baby. By his side was a smaller beam of light, flashing downward and then back up again. I showed the pictures to Darleen and then put them away. It was 1994. Today, those two photographs are displayed on the wall of my office, with another photo of a light beam that was directed into my sister's crown while we were vacationing in Hawaii a year after her brain surgery. One of these photos, the first Reiki beam, is being shown for the first time publicly in these pages. I think it was for *this very purpose* that it was "given" to me in the first place.

As I continued with my Reiki classes, my days became very structured around practicing Reiki, preparing written material for the Reiki classes I would be teaching, and caring for Mom. My first Reiki class was held in my parents' dining room! From the moment I dedicated my life to teaching Reiki, I have never been without a group of students ready and willing to learn. In addition, I have never been interrupted during a Reiki class by a phone call or a visitor. In fact, it seems as though time stands still and all becomes very quiet while class is in session. I like to tell my students that the angels are holding the space. (I know this to be true.) Furthermore, I was never interrupted while writing these pages for you. As weird as this sounds, please know that my life's "busyness" is put on "hold" while I fulfill my divine purpose in teaching my Reiki classes and in sharing these stories with you. As you discover and begin to fulfill your own divine purpose, I promise you'll have the same or a similar experience. God surrounds us with angels and a blanket of peace when we allow time and space to fold within us as we endeavor to answer His call. *Our task is great. Remember who we are. Burn with desire for the restoration of our spiritual selves and experience ourselves, once again, Home with God.* For me, Reiki was the ticket.

Reiki didn't originate in Japan, but its name came from the healing center founded by Dr. Mikeo Usui in Japan in the late 1800s. Mrs. Takata, a patient from Hawaii who traveled to his clinic, learned the technique in Japan in the mid-1900s and brought it to Hawaii where, years later, it was taught to, among others, William Rand. "Reiki" means "spiritually guided universal life force energy." This is a literal translation for "God directing Humanity." When I surrendered my life to God after completing my Reiki training, holding nothing back, I found that my life was now being gently "guided" with a sense of calm and focus that I had never experienced before. Of course, I've still experienced a few ups and downs over the ensuing years, but I can see that my train (life) has not derailed and that it is definitely headed somewhere intentional. (Thus, *"divine ordinance."*) With this perspective, life for me has become an adventure rather than a challenge.

While in the midst of my esoteric studies and activities, another blessing was about to be bestowed, this time upon myself and my sister . . .

# The Truest Measure

When the wellspring appears to have gone dry
And the walls of my mind are painted in lackluster
And spirit seems to have vacated for a warmer climate
I'm called upon to find my truest measure

When inspiration dangles on the breeze
And wafts a hint of longing in the air
Enticing me to notice how mundane I have become
I'm called upon to demonstrate I care

The saddest thing I've encountered
On this quest of bringing Spirit into expression
Is not the lack of finding what I want
But finding a lack of want

# DOT'S ANGEL

It was Thanksgiving, 1995. Darleen and I had just cooked a huge Thanksgiving dinner for our family of about 20 people when I heard Him speak to me as I was taking the turkey out of the oven. (What is up with those stoves?) Audibly, He said, "*Take a plate to Dot.*" I kid you not! I'm just about to serve Thanksgiving dinner to a large group of people and suddenly I'm being told to take a plate to a woman I haven't seen in 32 years! I was only 13 years old the last time I saw Dot. I had no clue if she was even still alive. She would be in her 80s by now. And what if she had moved? I looked at my sister, Darleen, who was helping me remove the turkey from the oven, and said, "Wanna go for a ride?"

"Yep!" She was grinning.

We quickly prepared a plate in a basket for Dot, placed the rest of the food on the table, called everyone to dinner, and then announced that we'd be back in an hour or two. No one, not one person, objected. They all just smiled at us and started eating, like they were all in on this little escapade!

The drive out to Dot's was eerie. There wasn't another car on the road the whole way there. It took a while, about 45 minutes, to get to the town where she had lived when we last saw her. Since I had been a kid the last time I had been out there, I wasn't even sure if we had the right road. I remembered that it had been a country lane, adjacent to a canal. Turning onto a small lane just before the canal, we tried to find a small farm that might look familiar. Darleen, who is six years younger than me, had an even dimmer memory of Dot's house. Finally, we found the farm, though it looked smaller than we remembered.

We followed the driveway to the rear of the property. Two small dogs barked at us from inside the yard, which was surrounded by a chain-link fence. We sat silently in the front seat of my giant Gladiator van. The windshield was tinted. Anyone looking up and into the vehicle probably wouldn't be able to see us at all. For a moment, I felt foolish. I considered retreating. Suddenly, a tiny, red-haired woman came from the rear of the house and strolled through the yard, hushing the barking dogs. Looking up at my windshield from a distance of at least 20 feet, she called out, "Darleen? Janet? Is that you?"

We didn't have time to cry. How could Dot have known that sitting in the strange vehicle in her driveway on Thanksgiving Day would be her old friend's two daughters whom she hadn't seen in over 30 years? Especially since she couldn't even *see* us through the tinted windshield? We piled out of the vehicle and rushed to Dot, hugging her and explaining that we had brought her a Thanksgiving dinner. Dot cried, but only for a brief moment. She was so happy to see us. While she ate, she told us that her family had called her just a short while before and had explained that they wouldn't be able to spend Thanksgiving with her. Instead, they would be arriving the next day. They were traveling from Oregon and their car had broken down. Dot was just about to cook macaroni and cheese for her Thanksgiving dinner. Worse, she would have had to eat alone. (Her husband, Joe, had passed away many years before.)

We visited for a while, giving Dot a brief history of Mom's life since the two women had last seen each other. Dot shared her story with us, too. She had recently undergone a double mastectomy. Like an innocent child, she pulled up her tee-shirt and showed us her scars. I felt absolutely no repulsion whatsoever. (I always thought I would be repulsed by that particular sight.) I only felt honored by her spirit and bravery. She was 83 years old and still had the spirit of a young woman! After our visit, we promised to bring Mom out to see her the following week and then we headed home. Dot thanked us profusely and kissed us good-bye.

Heading home to our own Thanksgiving dinner, Darleen and I barely spoke until we got to an intersection in a tiny rural town about ten minutes into our drive. Suddenly, Darleen started yelling, "Pull over, Janet! Look! It's an angel!" I pulled the van off of the road and onto a vacant lot and leaned over to Darleen's window. In the sky, filling up the entire western hemisphere, was a magnificent angel in all of her splendor! She was not made of clouds. She was real. She was smiling at us and turning her head to emphasize that she was living and breathing, blessing us with gratitude for listening to Him and for bringing a small measure of joy to one of His children. Her robes were flowing with color—white, magenta and violet. Her wings were enormous, spreading for miles. She was the most beautiful thing we'd ever seen.

I looked around for witnesses. Another van had pulled off the road behind us. The entire family had gotten out of their vehicle and were watching the angel, hands shielding their eyes from the sun, fingers pointing to where she was appearing in the sky, expressions filled with amazement. I grabbed my camera and took a picture of the angel. After that, I have no memory. I don't remember driving home, eating dinner, anything. The afternoon had been too much for me.

When the photos were developed, the one of the angel was missing. I was heartbroken. I would have loved to have included it here. At least I have Darleen as a witness. Whenever I tell this story to a naysayer, I just have them call my sister and she confirms the entire story! Thank God she was there! Someday, we'll see our angel again. There's not a shadow of a doubt in my mind. She'll be standing near the doorway to *Home with God . . .*

# The Visit

*It has been six months since I was asked to share this experience with you*
*The Visit*
*He knew it would be difficult for me, but the goal is far greater than the cost*
*So I began to tell the story, at first to just a few,*
*My closest friends, my students, and now you*

*Four times I felt the shift in vibration*
*It was startling, stunning; everything was dancing!*
*All became pure energy, shimmering, even the air*
*I lost consciousness, deeply, only to be awakened by the presence*
*Of the highest frequency I could withstand*
*Surrounding me in its radiance, time after time*

*Then, He appeared, swept into the room from above*
*With a velocity only He could carry*
*Embracing me like a small child as He folded me into His arms*
*Sealing every inch with His garment of golden fabric*
*I knew His presence from past meetings; once I had even touched His cheek*
*But never did I expect to be lifted from my sleep*
*And swept through the ceiling into flight*
*Bundled in the arms of the One I loved the most*
*How? Why?*

*First, I had to ask to see His face, although there was really no need*
*His Presence is unmistakable*
*And of course, I questioned Him by name, "Jesus?"*
*"Yes." His voice is Truth itself*
*Peace beyond description envelopes everything, everywhere*
*Even my voice echoes softly into eternity*
*We soar past the outer universe until we reach the inner*
*Where time and space fold into Now and Forever*
*The place where living stops and Life begins*

*Along the way to the edge of time we speak of the urgency*
*With which I am beckoned; how this came to be*
*Four reasons are offered in response to my need to know*
*First, He tells me, is the drama, which is being played out on Earth as we speak*
*The recreation of events from His Life*
*I had witnessed this play of drama two months earlier, in a dream*
*Now, I knew why*
*Second, the baptisms, offered with love during our services*
*Third, my work, a service of sharing in total dedication to God*
*And fourth, the message of love from the Emissaries of Light*
*As told to us by Twyman, the Peace Troubadour*
*A man who speaks the Truth to all who listen*

*For two days before the Visit, I had been sharing the message*
*With all who assembled*
*For two years before that, I had been pointing the direction*
*For those who knew themselves to be ready*
*And now, with the blanket spread and the date set*
*I'm summoned for a visit to the other side of perception*
*The memory of the meeting is sealed inside my mind*
*Waiting for the moment to come, when we all remember*
*What has long been forgotten—the Truth*
*As it is revealed to each of us*
*When we Visit*

# THE CENTER

The next spring, I enrolled at a local state university to earn the 90 credits I still needed as a pre-requisite for entering acupuncture school. It would take about two years of attendance as a full-time student. Unfortunately, a short time later, my sister was diagnosed with a brain tumor. I moved in with her and helped as much as I could while still attending school. She underwent surgery and then was put on bed-rest for several months. The tumor was inoperable, but a shunt was installed to minimize her symptoms. In spite of this, Darleen bounced back in record time and signed up for summer camp as a counselor. (She has worked as an educator her entire adult life and has summers off.)

Mom was doing much better in those days, so I grabbed the opportunity to complete my training. After two years at university, I would be traveling to the Bay Area three days a week to study acupuncture for another three years. Then, my mission would be accomplished. It was during the summer break of my second year at university that I received a visit from my Reiki guide, Tara.

Two years earlier, he had appeared to me in a full-blown vision while I was listening to the "Meet Your Reiki Guide" meditation by William Rand during my First and Second Degree Reiki weekend class. I was feeling exhausted from studying the First Degree Reiki symbols until 3:00 a.m. the night before. At the same time, I had watched my four-month-old nephew while my sister and her husband attended their high school reunion. During the Second Degree class the next day, I was having trouble paying attention to my teacher, Jeanette, and I silently hoped that she would begin a group meditation so that I could fall asleep for a while. When she finally put on the meditation tape, I sank into a deep sleep. Mid-way through, I felt my body rapidly vibrate up to a much higher frequency. Suddenly, there appeared a beautiful man standing in front of me, looking into my eyes. He was wearing a brown robe, tied at the waist with a braided cord. His hair was brown, shoulder length and slightly wavy. Around his head, situated mid-way down his forehead, he wore another braided cord, tied in the back. I couldn't determine a nationality. He was just beautiful to me. He said only three brief sentences, *"Hello. My Name is Tara and I will be your Reiki guide. You will know my presence when you feel pressure at your temples."*

I sat bolt upright, looking around to see if any of the other Reiki students could see Tara. Their eyes were closed and they had serene, peaceful expressions on their faces. I couldn't tell if he had appeared to any of them. Later, when I questioned them, I realized that I was the only one who had seen him. Each of the other students had been shown, in their own fashion, an impression of their Reiki guide, but none of them described Tara.

Over the next few years, I would spend a fair amount of time exploring the "inner planes" on spiritual travels with Tara. In his company, I could fly like a bird with wings. We spoke occasionally but briefly. His voice was distinct, but without accent. There was a tinge of an echo mixed with precise clarity. Usually his statements were direct and to the point, like the one he made the day I was on summer break from school, *"Come on, Jan. You're opening your healing center now."*

I had been meditating deeply, listening to an eight-directional Tai Chi meditation tape, when Tara virtually appeared, standing next to the couch I was lying on. As he spoke, he lifted my hand. Shocked that Tara was asking me to open my healing center now—before I was finished with school—I jumped off of the couch and blurted, "I can't open a healing center now. I still have three more years of acupuncture school left!" At this point, I could no longer see him, but I could still hear him and feel his presence. My frequency had dropped when I came abruptly out of the meditation. Fortunately, I could still hear him clearly, *"You're opening your healing center now and it will be one block from . . . (here he named a fast-food restaurant downtown)."* All I could think at this point was how could my Reiki guide know this? Has it already been decided, on another level, that I will be opening my healing center now? Even before I finish my training? And he even knows where the center will be located? I had already opened a healing center once before, back East. I knew how much money it would take to establish a new business and how long it would take for me to save that much. To open my center in New Jersey, I had saved half of my paychecks for a year! I didn't have that kind of money put away yet for the opening of a healing center here! How was I supposed to do this?

Inviting my grandson, Michael, and his friend, Mike, to go with me for a coney-dog, I drove to the restaurant and parked my car in a stall. The server skated out to us and took our order. By the time it was served, I had convinced myself that Tara had not actually visited me during my meditation and I did not, in fact, need to find a property to house my healing center. Finishing my drink, I was about to pull out of the stall and drive home when Michael said, "Um, Grandma? We're not just here for a coney-dog, are we?"

Wide-eyed, I asked, "Why are we here, Michael?"

"We have to find you a house!" He was smiling from ear to ear. He knew that I lived with my sister in the house our father had built and that I didn't need to find another residence. How could he know that I was there to look for a property? I hadn't uttered a word to the boys about the reason for this visit on the drive over.

"Yes, Michael," I sighed, "We have to find me a house." *OK, Tara. You win!*

The property we found was only three doors from the restaurant, on the same street. It was zoned for commercial use, although, like most of the neighborhood, it had been built as a single-family home many years before. Within days, I was scheduled to meet with the owner, who wanted to sell the property to me for a song. Everything was falling into place without a hitch.

During this time, my nephew, Brandon, and I were also planning a surprise birthday party for his mom, Darleen. She was turning 40 that Saturday. Our entire family of 45 members was planning to surprise her at 8:00 p.m. as she and I returned home from her usual birthday gift from me—a steak dinner at her favorite restaurant. I had arranged to meet with the real estate broker and the owner of the new property early that same afternoon at 2:00 p.m. I was getting ready for the meeting when the phone rang.

It was the broker, explaining that his wife wanted to leave a couple of hours early for a vacation and that he would meet with me the following week, if that was OK. I had worked in real estate before and I knew that it would be extremely rare for a broker to postpone the signing of contracts on a commissionable deal for a week based on just leaving a couple of hours early for vacation. Too many things can happen that could upset the sale. As he spoke, I found myself bathed in white light. I knew that this house was the wrong property for my center. Even as I agreed to meet with them in a week, I knew that I would never actually meet these people. Something else was waiting in the wings.

That night, I found the "something else." As Darleen and I were starting the salad course at her birthday dinner, I silently calculated how much time I could devote to each course and, if necessary, a glass of wine afterward so that we would arrive home for her surprise party at exactly 8:00 p.m. Our niece, Cheri, had baked a cake with black frosting and ribbons as a gag for celebrating Darleen's "over-the-hill" birthday. Mylar Grim Reaper balloons and black crepe paper decorated the living room walls. Over-the-hill gag gifts were mixed in with her real gifts. We were a rotten crew, planning a surprise party with an over-the-hill theme for a woman just turning 40! Oh, to be 40 again and to know what I know now! Ah well, I digress . . .

During the second course of our birthday dinner, my sister suddenly tapped her fingers on our table and said, "Now, let me tell you what I want for my birthday."

Stunned, I replied with as much authority as I could muster, "You're already getting your birthday gift—this dinner!" I couldn't let on about the party, but I was worried that she might be thinking we could go to a movie after dinner.

"I know. You always take me to dinner for my birthday, but I want to go to a book-signing, too."

Trying to look unruffled, I asked, "What book?" I was beginning to panic. This detour to a bookstore could derail our arrival to the party by 8:00 p.m., even if I cut out the dessert and wine!

"Soul Travel." She was smiling broadly.

"What? You hate that stuff! You're more into aliens and UFOs!"

"No, I'm not! I like it now!" She had the defiant tilted chin thing happening. I wasn't going to be able to talk her out of this. Plus, if I seemed to object too much, she might figure out that 45 people were preparing to give her the surprise birthday party of her life.

"OK," (trying to keep a poker face,) "so, who wrote the book?" I couldn't ask where or when. She might get suspicious if I seemed too concerned about time.

"Albert Taylor."

"Never heard of him." I dropped the subject, sure that if we left the restaurant a half-hour earlier than planned we could stop by the bookstore, stand in line for 20 minutes or so and still arrive home by 8:00. I forewent the glass of wine. Leaving the restaurant, I asked Darleen where the bookstore was.

"I'll show you," she said, and proceeded to direct me around town in a blind maze of haphazard turns. Finally, we pulled up in front of a Berkeley-style building on a tree-lined street that felt oddly familiar.

Getting out of the car, I turned toward a property on the next block. It was the restaurant Tara had directed me to. Suddenly, Darleen grabbed my arm and, pointing to a seemingly-vacant building next door to the bookstore, said, "What's going on over there?"

"I don't even know where I am, let alone what's going on in that place!" I replied in surprise.

"Well, maybe you'd better find out!" she said coyly and flounced into the bookstore without waiting for me. Entering the bookstore, I located the owner and asked him if he knew anything about the building next door. He explained that it was his building and that it would be going up for rent since the previous occupant, a chiropractor, had moved to another location only days before. I rented the building that very night.

While my sister listened intently to a lecture by Albert Taylor, I called home to see if I could postpone the party for an hour. The book-signing was actually a *lecture/*book-signing! "Hurry!" my niece Cheri whispered, "The guests are all here!" Not knowing what else to do, I interrupted Albert in front of 50 people and asked him to take a break so that my sister, who was sitting adoringly at his feet, and I could leave. I tried to bluff an excuse to leave by claiming that I had a migraine headache. Knowing that I had never had a headache in my life, Darleen looked at me incredulously and told me to shut up and sit down! Now, I had no choice. I blurted out the truth to Darleen about her surprise party in front of Albert and his entire audience. At the time, I don't think she believed me. Taking pity on me and my plight, Albert invited Darleen to come back the next day at 2:00 p.m. and he would sign her book. Reluctantly, and still yelling at me, she agreed to let me drive her home to her party. I made her swear that she'd act surprised when everyone jumped out at her. Actually, she was flabbergasted when it happened. She still didn't believe there was a surprise party waiting for her and almost had a heart attack when she walked through the door to be accosted by 45 people jumping out from hiding while screaming "Surprise!"

The next day, Albert signed Darleen's book as promised. She brought home a copy of his book for me as well. It was so refreshing to read about "out-of-body" experiences from a man who had been a NASA scientist for 17 years! Here was someone actually publicly admitting that he traveled to other dimensions regularly! (In those years, I was very secretive about my "travels," except with close friends and family.)

A series of events occurred after Darleen's birthday that can only be chalked up to synchronicity, serendipity or divine intervention. Not only did I find the right property for my healing center, but Albert's life was changed forevermore, as well! No one but Albert knew, but his days of book-signings were ending the night of his lecture at the bookstore. He was planning to go back to work at NASA after this last event, since the book tour had been unsuccessful. Unaware of any of this, my sister, a short time later, recommended to Art Bell, the then-host of the late-night radio talk show, "Coast to Coast," that he e-mail Albert after Art had mentioned on the air that he had never had a guest on his show who had experienced an "out-of-body" journey.

It was well after midnight. Darleen, who is always listening to the program as she sleeps, sat bolt upright and e-mailed Albert's address to Art, telling him about Albert's book. A couple of weeks later, Albert was a guest on Art's show. Instantly, his book became a best-seller. Over the ensuing years, he has been a frequent guest on Art's show and has since written several more books. This might never have happened had Darleen not attended his lecture on her birthday! I love how *Spirit* links events together for the highest good when we're finally willing to say *"yes"* to these adventures!

As for the funding I needed to open my new healing center—a few days after I rented the building with a deposit, I spent a late afternoon sitting on the bare floor of the living room, sketching out my plans for the business. By the hazy light of dusk, I calculated how much money would be required to prepare for the scheduled opening on September 15, 1996. It was now August 10. In less than six weeks, I would need to put together the funds necessary for the first and last month's rent, utility deposits, a business license, basic furnishings, advertisements, and, if possible, carpeting for the main room. There were three rooms for massage therapy, a large (living) room for Reiki classes, which would also double as a waiting room, a screened-in porch for merchandise and a kitchen for my office. The 1940s-era house had been converted for commercial use many years before. It even had a wheelchair ramp leading to the front porch. Still, my office was obviously a kitchen, (yes, with a stove . . .) but I liked the homey atmosphere. The counters and cupboards were perfect for storing essential oils and herbs. (In case you're wondering, I'm writing this book—where else?—in my kitchen!)

As I added up the funds necessary to bring the center to life, the front door suddenly opened. I watched, bewildered, as three women entered the room and made a semi-circle around me. I had never seen any of them before in my life. One of the women leaned over and spoke very softly to me, "We want you to teach us Reiki to the Master level and we're each going to pay you in full in advance." She then straightened up and, with the other two women, stood silently smiling at me.

"I'm sorry," I stammered, "What did you say?"

Sweeping her hand in front of all three of them, the woman repeated her statement, "We want you to teach us Reiki to the Master level and we're each going to pay you in full in advance." I was flabbergasted. In those days, students of Reiki paid $1,200 each for the full Reiki Master training. If these three women signed up for my classes and prepaid for the full course, they would be paying me $3,600—exactly the amount I had scribbled on my notepad for the healing center's start-up expenses!

I asked them how they knew I was there. Nothing on the building indicated that a new business was opening. I hadn't even posted a notice in the newspaper yet. They smiled and told me not to worry about it. They just wanted to sign up and pay in advance. I quickly assigned the class dates to them and accepted their money. Now, my healing center was a reality! The next day, I thanked the bookstore owner for the referral. He shook his head. The bookstore had been closed the day before. No one had been referred to me. Someone else must have sent them. But later, when I asked my new Reiki students who had sent them to me, they changed the subject. I never got an answer to my question!

Over the next decade, many events would take place that would mirror this serendipitous quality, especially events surrounding the eventual opening of my school. One such event occurred on a Monday afternoon while I was teaching a private Reiki class. I had just completed the introduction to Second Degree and was about to cover the Reiki "manifesting grid" when I heard a knock at the back door . . .

# KAUA'I

It was my sister, Darleen. I knew that her office was only a few miles from my center, but I was very surprised to see her stopping by on a workday unannounced. She had never done that before. "What are you doing here in the middle of the day? I asked, "Aren't you supposed to be at work?"

"Never mind that," she replied, waving her hand, "I need to ask you something."

"OK. Ask."

"I want to go to Hawaii."

She had a look on her face that I'd never seen before. In that brief moment, I knew what was happening. It had been only 16 months since her tumor was diagnosed. The projected life expectancy for someone with her type of tumor was five years. She had no way of knowing how many of those five years she would be able to travel. The one place she had always wanted to visit was Hawaii.

"Well, I'd like to go to Hawaii, too," I offered. "Do you have any money saved?"

She shook her head, "No. Do you?"

"No. My new business is just getting started."

"Well, how are we going to get there?"

"I don't know! Let's put it on the Reiki grid." Entering the Reiki room, I asked my student if it would be OK to show him the manifesting grid using my sister as an example.

"Sure!" he nodded. I then drew a circle to represent the earth on a large dry-eraser board. Inside the circle, I drew ocean waves, a palm tree, a setting sun, and stick figures to represent Darleen and myself. I wrote our names next to the figures and drew a little lei around each of our necks. Above our heads, I wrote, "Hawaii, 1997, Now, Fun, Laughter, Love," and the dollar sign, "$." Finishing, I drew a Reiki symbol—"Choku-Rei"—on the edge of the earth's circumference and then covered the circle with five "grid" lines, sweeping them all the way across the circle. Done, I stepped back so that Darleen could examine the grid.

Staring intently at the board, she folded her arms like a genie and nodded her head once quickly. (I swear I'm not kidding!) Then, she left the building and went back to work. Four days later, she called me at 7:30 in the evening. I was at home. I picked up the phone to hear my sister screaming, "We're going to Hawaii!! We're going to Hawaii!!" Within a week, we were boarding a flight to paradise. A local radio station had awarded an all-expense-paid trip to my sister and "a friend."

The trip consisted of three days and nights on Maui and four days and nights on Kaua'i. Checking into our hotel on Maui, we were informed by the desk clerk that we had been bumped from our room. Instead, we would be staying at a luxury condo resort property on the beach! We spent a beautiful three days relaxing and sight-seeing on Maui before flying to Kaua'i. The four days we spent on Kaua'i held a bit more adventure. We toured the island from inside out, exploring the canyons, beaches and caves. There was a spiritual energy on the island that felt very familiar to me.

I had experienced the same feeling in 1995, when I had spent my first vacation on Kaua'i with a friend. It had been evening. I was standing on the sand looking out over the ocean when I turned and looked up toward a bluff. There was a building atop the bluff, but it was too dark for me to make out the structure. Suddenly, I felt the property begin to draw a deep wellspring of longing out of my heart, like a powerful magnet pulling me to its walls. I had never felt such a pull before. It was as though I were a part of the building on the bluff and was being compelled to run to it. The next day, I drove up to the property and asked a crew of workmen what it was. I was hoping that it was a hotel and that I could book a room. They told me the property was condominium homes. Baffled, I left. It wasn't until two years later when visiting Kaua'i with my sister that I remembered the bluff again.

On our second day on Kaua'i, Darleen and I drove to the hotel below the bluff to attend a luau. We got there too late to eat, so we decided to sit on the beach for a while before heading out to dinner somewhere else. It was dark. The scene was exquisite—moonlight casting over the ocean waves, brilliant stars overhead, the exotic fragrance of tropical flowers. I never wanted to leave. Then, turning my head, I realized I was, once again, gazing upon that bluff! As suddenly as it had happened two years before, the property on the bluff reached out to me and began pulling my heart into it. Time stood still. I was enraptured with this far-away piece of the earth. Regaining my speech, I told Darleen about my intense attraction to the property on the bluff. It wasn't easy, but she talked me down and we finally left. With inexplicable sadness, I walked to the car and drove away. Before the night was over, I had again forgotten about the property on the bluff.

While in Kaua'i, two events took place that have had lasting effects on both my sister and myself. The first event occurred in the middle of the night, while we were both sleeping. I felt a pressure in the center of my forehead and awoke to see a large, dense beam of light moving toward me. As it entered the spot on my forehead where I had felt the pressure, I suddenly felt as if the top of my head was being (painlessly) blown off. I remember thinking, "I guess it'll be OK if I go home with half of my head gone!"

Instantly, there appeared a newborn baby inside of an oval frame just in front of me. I reached out and placed my hand into the oval, touching the baby's tiny hand. At that moment, the baby curled its fingers around my index finger, grasping it firmly. Awe-struck, I thought, "This baby is real and alive!" At that moment, I heard Christ's voice next to me, saying, "*The children born today are the Christ returning to earth.*"

It was August of 1997. The infant looked to be about two months old. Because of this experience, I believe that every child born on earth since June of 1997 is an "Indigo" child, with attributes of the "Christ" quality in their biology. Time will tell. As they age into adults, perhaps we'll see a generation of peacekeepers striving to restore harmony to our battle-weary world.

The second event occurred as Darleen and I were leaving our hotel for a luau on our last night in Kaua'i. Earlier, we had been shopping for souvenirs to bring home to our families. As the clerk was ringing up our purchases, Darleen suddenly pulled a disposable camera off of a counter display and included it with her purchase. I reminded her that we had two cameras and six rolls of film in the car.

"I don't care," she replied, "I want this one, too."

This was not like my frugal sister. The camera cost $20 and was obviously not a necessity. I knew something was up. A short while later, as we were walking across the hotel grounds to our rental car, I heard my Reiki guide's voice: *"Take a picture."*

Looking at Darleen, I asked, "Where's that camera?"

"Right here." She held up the new camera by its strap.

"Hurry," I instructed. "Give me the camera and go stand in front of that tree."

She obliged with a look of knowing and positioned herself next to the tree while I shot the only photo taken with that disposable camera. Later, when we arrived home, Darleen took all of the film in to be processed, including the disposable camera. The photo we took in front of the tree was the only exposed shot that developed. No other photos taken with our two cameras and the six rolls of film were developed. The exposures all came out blank. In the one good photo, a large beam of blue-green light is funneling into my sister's crown. I believe the beam of light was the Reiki beam, blasting my sister with healing Reiki energy, documented with a disposable camera that seemed at the time to be an extravagant purchase. Had we tried to shoot the photo with our own cameras, it would not have developed. Darleen's next MRI showed a blue halo inside the interior of her skull. Her neurosurgeon said that he'd never seen anything like it before. It has now been many years since that trip to Hawaii and Darleen's tumor has not increased in size. She is very much alive and filled with vitality.

Sylvia Brown, one of the world's foremost psychics, states in several of her books that we each choose five incidents that could potentially bring about our passing. As each incident approaches, we can choose to use it as an opportunity to move on or to wait for another of our five choices to present itself. The choice to wait is usually made if we feel that there is more we can learn in this lifetime. I believe that my sister's brain tumor was one of her choices and that she elected to stay in this lifetime longer out of her love for the children of our family, two of whom she has been raising since a few years after our Hawaii experience. Her choice to stay may have elicited the trip to Hawaii and the Reiki healing she experienced there. I guess, to find out for sure we'll have to wait until our past-life reviews before finally going *Home with God* . . .

The following year, I was again teaching a Second Degree Reiki class when I realized that my manifesting grid was outdated. I had been using the Hawaii grid I had drawn during Darleen's Reiki-class visit in 1997 to demonstrate how the process works. As I was recreating the original grid, I suddenly realized that I could bring the date forward to 1998 and really test the powers of manifestation with the results. You guessed it. Four days later, my boyfriend, who was also my center's bookkeeper, received a call from an old friend inviting us to join them on a trip to Honolulu! Our lodging had already been paid by another couple, who unfortunately had to back out at the last minute. We offered to reimburse them but they declined, telling us that if we just paid for the flight that they would be compensated enough. Back then, you could transfer flight fees. I was soon off on another adventure in paradise. It would be my third summons to my favorite piece of the earth—my bluff.

As soon as we arrived in Honolulu, I figured out why the other couple had backed out of the trip. Our hostess' husband suffered from bipolar disorder and had forgotten to bring his medications. He was a retired architect, and he quickly made it clear that he believed with a passion that we three members of his entourage wanted nothing more than to be personally toured by him through every high-rise building on Waikiki Beach. For two days, we walked on cement sidewalks into back door after back door, riding elevators and climbing stairs in order to view the inner workings of high-rise construction. I don't know how many chefs we startled or how many vacationing diners we disturbed. Finally, on the third morning, I met with our hostess' husband in the early morning as he was tying his sneakers for another long day of touring.

"Sweetie," I said in my most accommodating voice, "I think I'll sit this one out and just hit the beach today. My back is a little sore from all the walking and stair-climbing." You'd have thought I'd threatened to kill his dog! Waving his fists in the air, he started jumping up and down and screaming at me in an unintelligible barrage of words that sounded an awful lot like a toddler's tantrum. Only this toddler was over six feet tall! The others rushed into the room, wide-eyed. I lifted my hands in surrender and yelled, "Fine! I'll go with you! Calm down!" Instantly, he sat down, smiling, and resumed tying his shoes. I looked at his wife in exasperation. She explained again about forgetting his meds, apologizing profusely. As we began our long walk to Waikiki Beach, I swore that I'd never travel with people I didn't know very well ever again.

We began our tour, our hostess' husband walking down the street like a mama chicken with her baby chicks following behind. Already, my hostess and I had to sit on a bench for a minute to catch our breath. Then, catching up with the men about a block before reaching the main beach area, I began a series of actions that still stupefies me.

Without knowing why, I turned south and stopped in front of a beautiful high-rise building. I had stepped in front of the others when I turned and they followed me without question. The building had no external signs or markings. It was modern and sleek, with chrome windowsills and granite walls. I ran into the building and asked a young girl in the lobby, "Are they selling timeshare in here?" There was absolutely no reason for me to be asking this question. It was as though I had become someone else with an agenda I knew nothing about!

"Yes," the girl replied, "on the fifth floor."

I jumped into the elevator, rode up to the fifth floor and opened a door in the hallway marked "Embassy Suites" that was directly across from the elevator. Sticking my head into the room, I said to the receptionist, "Are you people selling timeshare in here?"

Eying me warily, she answered, "Yes."

"Great!" I exclaimed, "Put me on paper fast! I only have a few minutes. There's a whacko on the street!" I'm sure my frantic expression added to the drama. I was terrified that my hostess' husband would find me in this office and let loose with another raging tantrum. For some unfathomable reason, I needed to purchase a timeshare quickly, within minutes. If you've ever been to a timeshare presentation, you probably know that it's a 90-minute process and you can't be "put on paper" in just a few minutes. Still, I persisted.

The receptionist looked around and, spotting a manager, whispered something into his ear.

Eyebrows raised, he approached me and said, "I'm sorry, ma'am, but you would need to take a tour before we could 'put you on paper.' Do you have a little more time to spend for that?"

"I would love to take a tour but I don't have time. Just prepare the paperwork and I'll sign it. We have to do this fast. There's a nutcase on the street!"

Eyebrows raised a tad more, the manager lowered his head, looked sternly at me over his glasses and said quietly, "Nutcase?"

"Yes! He forgot his meds and I can't be gone for more than a few minutes! Please, we're wasting time. I promise I know what I'm doing. Just get the contracts ready for me to sign so I can get out of here before he throws another tantrum!"

I looked frantically at the door, expecting my hostess' husband to blaze through it at any moment screaming like a banshee. Instead, the door opened slowly and my three companions entered the room quietly. Then I realized—this was a high-rise! He won't throw a fit in a high-rise! He probably thinks I'm doing this for him! Looking at the three of them, I asked, "These folks would like to give us a tour. Is that alright?" Heads nodded all around. I took a deep sigh of relief, saying to the manager, "OK, we'll tour."

The manager assigned all four of us to a salesperson who seated us at a table and then promptly began pitching the sale to the older couple. I became agitated. I was the one demanding to be put on paper and now she was talking to the wrong couple! I was just about to walk out of the building when the manager stepped to my side and bent to whisper in my ear, "I know what you're doing but I can't put you on paper unless you see the property. How many days do you have left on your trip?"

"Five," I said.

"And who are you with?"

Pointing at my boyfriend, I said, "Him." Pointing at the older couple, I said emphatically, "Not them!"

"OK," he said, "here's what we'll do. I'm sending you and your boyfriend in a limousine to pick up your things from your hotel and then drive you to the airport. We're going to fly you to the resort and you'll spend the next five days and nights there. We're also going to pay for your rental car. If you fall in love with the resort at the end of your stay, we'll send your salesperson over to the island to go over the contracts with you before we fly you home. How does this sound?"

"Great!" I was relieved. "By the way, which island is the resort on?"

"You don't know?"

"No." I had no clue why I was even there, let alone which resort they were selling.

"Kaua'i."

"Kaua'i? Cool! What's the name of the resort?"

"Turn around." He motioned behind me. I shifted in my seat and turned my head toward a large mural on the back wall. There, in full display, spread out over a twelve-foot-wide area, loomed my Kaua'i bluff! The property was a timeshare, not condos! I could swear I heard the hauntingly beautiful music from the 1950s movie/musical set in Kaua'i, "South Pacific," from the scene where the camera slowly pans to the mystery island, "Bali Hai." Drawn into this sales office without obvious reason, I was now buying a piece of the property that had captivated my heart for three years!

Since then, I have visited Kaua'i almost every year, often with groups of family, friends and co-workers from the school. Always, the guests who travel with me are perfectly suited for the exact ceremony I am called to perform once I am there. Each visit is unique. The island offers many sacred ceremonial sites, long used by the island's ancestors to pray for humanity's restoration of *Spirit*. In the near future, I plan to organize larger group trips for extended stays on Kaua'i, some for the purpose of holistic health training (the resort property owner has offered me a classroom for those occasions) and others for participation in global peace prayer ceremonies. Go to my school's web-site listed on the reference page of this book to view details. A future book revealing the Kaua'i story will include previous and future visits, some of which may include experiences involving you!

In 1999, I wrote a book of prose inspired by *Spirit* entitled *When the Bird Sings, Spirit Speaks* . . . (Those "speakings" are sprinkled throughout this book, usually between segments.) On the last day of my Kaua'i visit that year, I wrote this verse explaining how I felt about the island. I hope you feel a connection to Kaua'i when reading these words. If you do, you may want to join me on our next sojourn to paradise.

# The Last Day

My Kaua'i,
My heart breaks
Every time I have to leave you.
Knowing this is the last day
I gaze out at your graceful curves
Your rugged coast
And rain-drenched palms
And listen to the music of your pounding surf.

Torches light the path
To your never-ending canvas
Of landscaped fantasy.
A world of misty waterfalls
And countless moments of forever
Wrapped in pristine splendor.
You fill me with all you have
Which is all I need.

I miss you even now
Before the packing begins.
Before the last sleep of exquisite dreams
When ancestors gather
To bid me farewell.
Before the fuchsia sunrise
In the still morning
Welcomed sweetly by eager birds
And a lone beach stroller
Making peace with paradise
On the last day.

# When the Bird Sings

*I no longer need awaken*
*When the bird sings*
*In the still darkness*
*Of the early morning*

*I no longer need to wonder*
*If this night will be the one*
*The harbinger of tidings*
*I hesitate to hear*

*So long, I gave notice*
*To the prospect of the call*
*Dreading news of relief*
*While praying for the best*

*Unsure which way to hope*
*Yet knowing that the moment*
*Reaches in without your bidding*
*When the bird sings*

# MOM'S LAST DAYS

The one thing I regret the most about Mom is that I never took her to Hawaii—her one unspoken passion. She and my dad had been married with the Hawaiian Wedding Song playing in their ceremony. In her youth, Mom had even been a hula dancer for a summer. Unfortunately, by the time I purchased my membership in the Kaua'i property, Mom was too ill to travel. Confined to her bed, she and my step-father lived in an assisted living complex near my home. By 1999, Mom had undergone a double mastectomy and eight rounds of chemotherapy. In January, her doctor told us that she would not survive another round because her heart was too weak. She now had about two weeks left to live. She was told to go home and make peace with her family.

Finally, I was free to use any and all holistic health protocols I chose for my mother. I was told that it wouldn't make a difference—she was dying anyway. She weighed about 80 pounds. Her skin stretched thinly over her skeleton. I could easily pick her up; she felt like a child. Although Mom couldn't see, her hearing was unimpaired. Every day, she listened to the entire movie, "Titanic," as it played on the TV in her bedroom. To the end, Mom was a hopeless romantic.

The moment she came home from her last hospital stay, I began to administer her natural health protocol. Each morning, I prepared her food and a "cocktail" for the day. Since I lived only three blocks from her, I could easily prepare her meals and deliver them to her on my way to work at the institute. All of her food was prepared from scratch.

Her bread was baked in a home bread-oven, using whole-grains. Her meals were cooked in a crock-pot—even meat loaf—to preserve all of the nutrients at low temperatures. She ate beef stews, her favorite, often. I loaded them with beef, vegetables and potatoes to provide as many calories as possible for the energy she would need to restore her vitality. She also drank a vitamin shake daily for additional nutrients and calories. Since she had lost all of her teeth, I slow-cooked everything to a very soft texture. Never a very feeble person, Mom loved to sit in her rocking chair and rock with glee while "gumming" her meat-loaf sandwiches. She was healing and she knew it.

Her daily "cocktail" was made very carefully in the morning, using the following recipe. I was guided intuitively, combining the method I had used in 1972 for my throat tumor with information I had learned later as a holistic health practitioner. The brew is actually very simple and contains easily available kitchen items.

## *Mom's Cocktail*

*Green Tea (in a tea bag)*
*2 cups charcoal-filtered water (not bottled)*
*½ t. freshly ground cinnamon*
*½ t. freshly ground cloves*
*½ t. freshly ground nutmeg*
*½ t. freshly ground black walnut hull (green hull—from a health-food outlet)*
*½ t. freshly ground wormwood bark (from a health-food outlet)*
*1 t. honey (local, 100 % pure honey)*
*1 heaping t. powdered Vitamin C (about 5,000 mg.)*
*1 cup apple cider*
*Juice of ½ fresh lemon*

In a drip coffee maker using an unbleached filter and the filtered water, brew the green tea, cinnamon, cloves, nutmeg, black walnut and wormwood. While the brew is still hot in the carafe, stir in the honey. Allow to cool to room temperature. (A couple of ice cubes help cool the brew.) Add the cider, lemon and powdered Vitamin C. Pour into a large

Thermos, adding a couple more ice cubes, if preferred. Drink slowly throughout the day. Repeat daily. This recipe has no known adverse side effects as recommended. Please do not modify it. To save time, you can purchase the cinnamon, cloves and nutmeg already ground from your local health-food outlet. The vitamin C, honey, green tea, charcoal filter and cider can also be purchased at most health-food outlets, as well as your local grocery store or pharmacy. The cocktail can be stored in a pitcher in the refrigerator instead of a Thermos, if you like.

Be sure to check with your physician before ingesting this or any herbal recipe in case of contraindications with other medications. It is also advisable to take a colon-cleansing supplement while using this recipe. This will flush out any debris stirred up from the herbs. If you experience discomfort, reduce the colon cleanser by half.

Skip the cocktail one day per week. When you feel it is time to cut the recipe down to three times per week, do so. Your body knows what it needs. Eventually drop the cocktail down to once or twice per week, or whenever you feel a need for it. If you have any known allergies to any of these ingredients, omit that ingredient.

Once prepared, I poured Mom's cocktail into an aluminum Thermos to keep it out of the sunlight, which could dissipate the nutrients. Mom would sip her cocktail throughout the day. As she did, she gained weight and overall strength until she became too heavy for me to lift. Her vision improved, although her sight was mostly in shadows. This greatly enhanced her daily viewings of "Titanic."

Within four months, Mom had gained 40 pounds, grown back a full head of lustrous hair, could walk back and forth to the bathroom on her own and had convinced my step-dad to take her out to lunch and dinner on a regular basis. She was nothing short of amazing! I still delivered her daily cocktail and some meals, also spending a few minutes each visit to give her a Reiki treatment or attunement. By May, Mom was almost her old self again, even visiting a local cosmetic counter to purchase her favorite make-up to wear to her Mother's Day breakfast.

That Sunday, on Mother's Day, I awakened to the sound of a beautiful female voice, telling me to get a pen and paper. The voice had a pink/peach coloration in its tone. (I associate or "see" colors with letters and words.) I dashed into the living room, startling my room-mate, who knew that I usually woke up in a groggy haze, and grabbed the pen and paper before sprinting back to my bed. Sitting in the middle of my bed, I wrote the words as "she" spoke them to me. It took about two hours, altogether, to record her message. I call it "The Messenger of Love."

# The Messenger of Love

*Years passed before I remembered*
*How to speak to you*
*How to help you listen*
*To the sacred messages of the*
*Language of Love*
*Come, draw near to me*
*I'll wrap this blanket of words*
*Around your shoulders*
*As your Spirit remembers*
*It won't take long*
*Not nearly as long as the waiting*

*This birth will be with great ease*
*No pain*
*No stress*
*No expense*
*The baby is already here, smiling*
*She isn't hungry or frightened*
*She has dancing eyes and golden hair*
*And nurses sweetly*
*She is you; she is me*
*And she can see*

*Hold her in your arms, cradled*
*Feel the serenity, the love she*
*Has brought you*
*She is here*
*The Feminine Principle*
*Rejoice*
*You are no longer alone; in truth*
*You never were*
*She was always here, inside of you*
*Waiting to be born*

*The Messenger of Love*
*Speaks the Language of Light*
*To your spirit, your self*
*Hear her with your heart*
*She speaks so softly*
*So lovingly*
*Her gentle peace is eternal*
*It bathes your soul, like balm*
*She loves to kiss your cheek*
*And laugh a girlie laugh*
*Enticing you to smile more often*
*Like a favorite aunt would do*

*She weeps, too*
*Late at night, she sits in a chair*
*In a far corner of your room*
*And cries your tears*
*To lighten your load*
*We live in such a heavy world*
*She loves us so much she cries*
*Tears of pain and joy together*
*She holds vigil at our bedside*
*As a mother of the sleeping child*
*Slipped into a coma*
*Unable to grasp the door knob*
*That can free us from our confinement*
*Unaware that our dreams*
*Are creations of slumber*

*She has so much to tell us*
*Now that she is reborn*
*Come to us as a child*
*Child of God, Mother of God*
*Knowing how abandoned we felt*
*Washing our tears away*
*With tender kisses and hugs*

*Today is Mother's Day*
*And our birthday, all of us*

That night, I read "The Messenger of Love" to Mom as part of her Mother's Day gift. As I was leaving her bedroom, I suddenly remembered that I had forgotten to "Reiki" her. Tuning back around, I was dismayed to see Tara, my Reiki guide, with Archangels Michael and Gabriel standing next to my mother's bed, waving me out of the room. I was not supposed to give my mom Reiki that night. *She was going Home.* I was not to try to keep her here any longer. It seemed strange to me that Mom would let me rejuvenate her physical body for four-and-a-half months just to demonstrate that it could be done and then to head on *Home with God* anyway. I wondered how she would make her exit, now that she was so much healthier.

As it turned out, I didn't have to wonder for long. The next day, I was teaching a class on herbs to students at my institute when suddenly I heard the entire *Company of Heaven* say to me, *"We are bringing your Mother home with us now."* The words were accompanied by angelic song and rejoicing. Instantly, I witnessed my mom, radiant with joy, being escorted by Jesus on one arm and my father, Dave, who had been waiting for her for 40 years, on the other arm. Countless angels paraded beside and behind them. Mom was ecstatic. She was young and beautiful and was wearing a long, flowing white gown. They all passed right in front of me and walked into Heaven and out of my sight. As they faded from view, my hand came up and slapped my own face! The students stared at me with wide, unblinking eyes as I told them that my mother had just passed away.

I called my step-dad. He told me that Mom was in a coma. That morning, she had gotten all dressed up in one of her linen suits with matching purse and shoes (Mom was a Southern belle) and had visited her doctor in his office unannounced. After convincing him that she was, indeed, still alive and thriving, he determined that she could now handle another round of chemotherapy. As soon as the needle was inserted, Mom looked at my step-dad and said, "I think I'll just close my eyes now and die." She went immediately into a coma and passed away the next day. We were told that her heart just exploded.

At the funeral parlor, I sat between Darleen and my step-dad. Since Mom's arrangements had been made years earlier, there was only the selection of a casket left for us to consider. Mom had arranged to be buried near my dad in the cemetery located in the town where Dot lived. There was to be a closed casket and a graveside service. This would have been fine if Mom hadn't just spent the last four months getting beautiful. She must have had second thoughts on her exit strategy because she decided to join us at the meeting. As I was quietly sitting and listening to the funeral director read off the list of arrangements, my mother gently tapped me on the shoulder and whispered in my ear in her southern accent, "Janet!" Her tone was urgent. Now, I must tell you that I was not expecting to hear my mother's voice at her own funeral arrangement meeting.

"Ma?" I whispered over my shoulder. "Is that you?"

"Tell that woman that I want the Hawaiian Wedding Song played at my funeral." Not only was my mother standing next to me and speaking to me, she was planning her own funeral!

"Excuse me," I interrupted the funeral director, who was reading aloud the provisions of Mom's policy, "Could we play the Hawaiian Wedding Song at Mom's funeral?"

"What are you doing??" my sister whispered loudly to me.

"Mom wanted the Hawaiian Wedding Song played at her funeral."

"How do you know that?"

"She told me." (I'm not going to lie, if possible, but I'm sure as heck not going to tell all of these people that my mother is standing in the room talking to me as we speak!)

"When did she tell you that?" Darleen was not convinced.

"The last time I spoke with her." (Not lying . . . Everyone knew that I saw Mom almost every day, so it made sense that I might be relaying a request she had made beforehand.)

"You can bring a boom box and play the song at the graveside service," the funeral director chimed in. We all agreed and I assumed that Mom had gone back to Heaven. No such luck.

"Janet!" (Yikes! She's still here!) "Tell that woman that I want a chapel ceremony." (I guess graveside isn't going to suffice any longer. Mom now wants an open casket!)

"Ma?" I couldn't believe this myself! Again, I asked for Mom's request. Again, when Darleen demanded to know when Mom had asked me to make the request, I explained, "The last time I spoke with her."

Unfortunately, Mom's policy didn't provide for the cost of a chapel ceremony. Undaunted, I offered to pay for the chapel myself. Anything to get my mom off my shoulder. Literally. At the conclusion of the meeting, it was decided that I would provide the service (yes, I am also a minister) and that the use of the chapel would be *included at no charge.* I think at this point, Mom was talking to the funeral director!

That night, I wrote my first funeral service. I had performed many marriage ceremonies and baptisms, but had not yet been called on to provide the service for a funeral. My esoteric studies provided a template for all religious ceremonies, but it was a tad metaphysical for the small, mostly fundamentalist community my family resided in. I improvised as much as I thought necessary to bring the service to a more traditional tone.

The next day, I met with three of my sisters to distribute the ceremony to them, highlighting the sections that I had prepared for each of them to share at the service. They all three declined, explaining that they were too distraught over Mom's passing to stand up and speak before the room. Somewhat disgruntled, I agreed to perform the service solo, with the help of my unwitting brothers. I planned to give each of them a prayer from scripture to read at the podium.

That night, at around 2:00 a.m., I awakened to my mother's voice. "Janet! Get up! I don't like that ceremony you wrote. I need for you to change it."

"Ma, I'm exhausted. Just tell me the changes and I'll fix it in the morning." (The ceremony and funeral were scheduled for 9:30 a.m. the next day.)

"No you won't. I need you to get up and fix them now!"

"Ma, come on . . . just tell me the changes. I really need to get some sleep. I've had a rough week. My mother just died . . ."

"I can't help it. You can't use that ceremony the way it is and there's too many changes to remember. Now come on. Get up!" Staggering out of bed, I spread the entire beautifully formatted ceremony out on the living room desk. Over the next four hours, my mother instructed me, step by step, on the rewriting of her funeral service. I scribbled between the lines, around the edges and on the back of the pages until the script was exactly as she wanted.

At 6:00 a.m., I woke up my room-mate and asked him to reformat the entire ceremony on his computer while I went back to sleep for a couple of hours. His eyes were huge with surprise, but he didn't ask questions. By the time I woke up, the new ceremony was finished. At 9:00 a.m., I arrived at my sister's house, which was only a short walk from the chapel. Our family had decided to meet there and walk over to the chapel together. As I opened the front door, bedlam ensued.

Two of my sisters, Dorothy and Bobbie, were attacking me with the copies of the ceremony that I had given to them the day before, exclaiming excitedly that Mom had visited them during the night and instructed them to make the same exact changes that she had instructed me to make! All three of us compared our rewritten scripts. The changes were verbatim. In addition, she had instructed both daughters to help with the ceremony and showed them which part they would read. (Darleen was excused, as were my three younger sisters, Julie, Robin and Fonda. Mom knew that it would have been too emotionally difficult for them to participate.)

At the chapel, I opened the ceremony with "The Messenger of Love." My brother, David, read The Lord's Prayer. Our other brother, John, read the 23rd Psalm. Dorothy told heartwarming stories about Mom. One of them, describing Mom's love affair with wallpaper (she had once wallpapered a car) was hilarious, bringing laughter to Mom's many friends and family members present. Bobbie shared loving stories as well. I ended with a reading from Scripture.

Mom's casket was open. She was beautiful. Everyone filed past her, amazed at how beautiful and serene she looked, and then we all joined the long processional to the cemetery. Once there, I saw the funeral director step out of the hearse. She approached me, tears in her eyes.

"I am one of your family, now," she said. "You know, I don't ever attend the funerals of my clients. This is the only one I have ever attended. I had to. Your Mom is here with us, in spirit."

"Oh yes," I assured her, "I'm sure of that! She's been visiting me for days. In fact, she wrote her own service!"

Staring at me through misty eyes, the director told me, "Last night, I was dressing your Mom and talking to her at the same time when her song, the Hawaiian Wedding Song, began playing on the radio. In my life, I have never heard that song on the radio before. I knew that she somehow played that song just for me so that I would know that she was really hearing me and that she was still here, even though I couldn't see her. Now I think I can believe in an afterlife when before I was never sure. Thank you so much for bringing your mom to me." We hugged and then joined the others for the playing of the Hawaiian Wedding Song at Mom's grave.

Over the years, Mom has visited me and other members of our family on many occasions, often just to stroke our hair or whisper our name. Shortly after she died, Mom left a long-stemmed red rose on Darleen's kitchen counter in the early morning, a pre-arranged sign that she had promised to Darleen before she passed. The rose bush in Darleen's front yard was not blooming. No one else had been in the house the night before. A few months later, Mom spoke to me as I was preparing chicken and dumplings for her birthday party. It had been only three months since her death and my sisters and I had decided to honor her birthday with her favorite foods. As I was pressing the dumplings into the bubbling broth (of course, in my crock pot), I heard Mom's voice, "Janet, I'm so proud of you."

"Ma? Is that you?" The lights blinked. "Ma! What are you doing here? I saw you ride a white horse *Home!*" A few nights before, I had awakened to see her riding a white horse and wearing a white dress and shouting at me, "*Janet! Wake up! Look at me! I made it! I made it!*" The horse carrying my mom had lifted higher and higher into the sky and seemed to be moving toward a place of the highest spiritual advancement, like *Home With God.*

"I thought you were gone!"

"Well I *thought* I'd be invited to my own birthday party!"

Well, there you go. She could still pop in and visit us! I guess there's still much more to learn about *Home With God* . . .

# A COURSE IN MIRACLES

$M$any years ago, I heard about a study program called *A Course in Miracles*. Opening the Course's workbook for students, I read the first line of the first lesson, "Nothing in this room (on this street, from this window, in this place) means anything." I was a young mother. My children were playing in the room. They meant *everything* to me! Had I read further, I would have realized that *my children are everything to everyone!* They, you, I, *everyone* is/are the *Child of God*, and each of us matter far, far more than we could ever imagine, *to God and to each other*. Furthermore, *there is only one of us here!* Whoa, Seabiscuit! How can that be? Look at us. We're as separate as we can be! Aren't we? Well, quantum physics says no, we're not separate after all. Many of our world's leading physicists are well aware, due to advanced quantum sciences, that we are actually a *field of intention*, creating with our thoughts at every moment. Read *The Biology of Belief*, by Bruce Lipton, Ph.D., or *The Power of Intention*, by Dr. Wayne Dyer, or anything by Dr. Deepak Chopra.

Even though I had experienced myself as *one* with everything in existence while enveloped in the tube of *One* during the weeping willow tree experience in 1968, I still couldn't comprehend the *oneness* of my seemingly separate self with all of the other seemingly separate members of humanity. Finally, after years of pondering this question, I began to realize that my *perception* of the world was directed by ego, and ego's trademark is separation, division, polarity, and duality. Once I began to see the world through the lens of *Spirit,* I could begin to perceive humanity, myself included, as the *One Child of God*, experiencing him/

herself within this dream of creation as many, many (seven billion) individualized units of consciousness. Every time I have visited *Home With God,* I have perceived the many facets of our *One Self* as sovereign beings, still retaining our individuality while existing in the realm of *One,* the ultimate *Heaven*—*Home With God,* much as trillions and trillions of individual droplets of water collectively comprise the vast oceans. *We are Home With God right now.*

The simple tool that I have used in order to perceive myself as *one* with humanity is this: While looking into the eyes of everyone with whom I speak, I envision them as the *Child of God,* my *brother or sister in Spirit,* and say to them silently, "*You are the creator of the universe, the Child of God, and there is only one of us here.*" (Wait a minute! The creator of the universe? How does this make sense? I thought God created the universe!) Yes, God did create the universe, as we have long been taught. But it was *we* who created the dream in which *we believe* that we are living *only here,* in this world of matter, separate from Him. And our dream long ago became a nightmare for many people of Earth. Furthermore, I was shown on my last visit *Home With God* that He misses those of us who *still believe* that we're only here, in this dream, and not at *Home* with *Him.* As long as we allow our collective ego to hold this dream in place through the lens of separation, (which fosters fear, guilt, blame, etc.), our virtual-reality viewing of this dream will continue. And the glue our ego uses to hold this dream of illusion in place is judgment. When we judge ourselves and others as guilty, or less than *perfect, whole and complete,* we add depth and substance to the ego's glue. Compassion and forgiveness provide the solvent that dissolves the ego and its veil of illusion. A metaphor I like to use to explain this dilemma is as follows:

> Imagine that you and your family are about to sit down to dinner. One of the kids is still in the family room, watching a movie. The movie has become so realistic to the child that he has become mesmerized by it and cannot turn his eyes away from the screen. It's as though the child is in a coma and can't

hear you calling him to dinner. You know that your child is *safe at home*, but his attention is *completely elsewhere*.

Now imagine this scenario lasting for years. You and your whole family will probably spend a great deal of time trying to gently nudge the sleeping child's attention away from the movie (dream) so that he can be reunited with his loved ones. You may even find a way to send one of your other children *into* the movie to try to reach the lost child, who now believes the movie is *all that exists*.

Now consider how you would feel if your mesmerized child suddenly responds to your whispered pleas to wake up with a brief look of recognition in his eyes as he looks away from the screen for a moment. This would be a cause for celebration, as it is evident that the child is trying to *come out* of the dream and remember his true reality here at home with you. As quickly as he sees you, however, his attention reverts back to the movie/dream.

The **Course in Miracles** offers the solution to this dilemma. If enough people begin to read the Course and apply its lessons, we may be able to shorten the time humanity is side-tracked by the illusion of separation. Imagine how surprised I was when I woke up one night and found myself fully expanded into the *whole of the universe*, just hanging out with *all that is*, being *one* with everything, and then suddenly hearing the big, booming *voice of Spirit* say to me, "*You are the creator of the universe.*" I was . . . well . . . not believing I understood the meaning of His statement! Still, I pondered it deeply for some time. Then, out of the blue one day in 2004, I was browsing online at amazon.com for a new book by Dr. Wayne Dyer when suddenly an offer to purchase another newly published book at a discounted price appeared on the screen. The book was titled *The Disappearance of the Universe*, by Gary Renard. This *way* caught my attention.

If you haven't read or heard of *The Disappearance of the Universe*, please stop reading this book for a minute (and only for a minute!) and go to www.garyrenard.com. He will tell you, in a brief video, why he wrote a book that would shake up your perception of reality, as his book has surely done for many people. *Disappearance . . .* is intended to be an introduction to **A Course in Miracles**, as is this book, also. While you're reading this book, you will most probably experience yourself in the restored state of being *Home With God* for a moment or two, especially if you do the meditation exercises included. The same thing will probably happen while reading *Disappearance . . .* by Gary, as well as while you're reading **A Course in Miracles** (by the Foundation for Inner Peace) or any one of a myriad of books that speak to your *Spirit* rather than to your ego.

Our ability to experience ourselves *Home With God* is not limited to any one teaching. Remember, we are all *Home With God* right now. How we choose to look away from this dream that we're enmeshed in and restore ourselves to the *Greater Reality* of *Home* is up to us. It just seems to me that we can hasten our steps *Homeward* by also reading the Course. Give it a try. Groups of **A Course in Miracles** students are meeting right now all over the world. Go to www.acourseinmiracles. com for more information. You can also purchase the book on amazon. com. Obviously, I highly recommend it.

James Twyman, author of "Emissaries of Light," "Secrets of the Beloved," and many other magnificent works, co-founded The Spiritual Cinema Circle with Stephen Simon, a noted movie producer (*What Dreams May Come*) and Neale Donald Walsch, author of the *Conversations With God* series of bestselling books. In his early years, James studied **A Course in Miracles** before becoming the "Singing Peace Troubadour," a title bestowed upon him by the council of the 12 major religions of the world at their meeting in Assisi, Italy, in which James played a concert of music to which he had ascribed their most prominent prayers during a spiritual experience.

Go to www.beloved.com or link to James through our web-site listed on the reference page at the back of this book. Also, please check out www.spiritualcinemacircle.com for more information on how to create your own circle of light in your home or church. The last time

I attended a James Twyman concert, he was wearing the gold tunic previously worn by Nelson Mandela, who had passed it on to James when they met in South Africa a few years before. I can think of no higher honor.

# We Are Choosing Peace

*(sing to the melody of Beauty and the Beast)*

*Can you see the day firings will cease?*
*Weapons on the shelf, camaraderie a wealth*
*We are choosing Peace*

*Can you hear the sounds, chatter on the beach?*
*People without fear, everyone a peer*
*We are choosing Peace*

*Like a candle flame, no two are the same*
*Flickering our light, illuminating night*
*'Til we end this game*

*Can you smell the air, salt and foamy seas?*
*Savoring our lands, neighboring our hands*
*Offering the keys*

*Redwoods on the hills, cobble on the streets*
*Laughter in the skies, footsteps on the rise*
*We are choosing Peace*

# CHIEF JOSEPH

In the summer of 1999, I was teaching a Reiki Master class in my back yard when I first met Joseph. More than a decade before, I had been told by a clairvoyant friend that I was accompanied in spirit by a very tall Native American chief in full feather headdress. During the Reiki Master class, I was finally able to see him myself.

I had just begun the second segment of the Reiki Master attunement for eight students on the patio deck. At that time, I owned and resided in a historic gold-rush hotel/bed and breakfast in the Sierra foothills' town of Knights Ferry. Although my school was twelve miles away in Oakdale, I often held yoga and Reiki classes at the hotel, especially if my students were from out of the area and needed lodging. On this particular day, I decided to hold class outside in the warm sunshine.

By the time I had begun the third student's attunement, a car's horn suddenly began blaring repeatedly in my parking lot a few feet away from where we were holding class. The only student who seemed to notice this was the owner of the car. She quickly rushed into the house to retrieve her keys while I stood silently waiting. I was quite surprised by the intrusion. Until that day, I had never been interrupted in the slightest manner during a Reiki attunement. Closing my eyes, I looked into the inner planes for a reason. Suddenly, my inner vision opened up onto the hotel's grounds just beyond the Reiki circle of students. There, forming a semi-circle around my class, stood a Native American chief in full feather headdress and a dozen or so younger warriors. I felt honored by their presence. Assuming (erroneously) that these regal visitors had come to our meeting to receive healing, I said, in spirit, to the Chief, *"Hello."* (The car's horn had ceased honking the moment the Native Americans became visible to me.) *"Are you here to receive healing from us?"*

*"We are here to offer healing to you."* (Oops! How right they are when they say never to "assume" or you might make an "ass of you and me.")

*"Oh, yes!"* I stammered, *"Of course! Thank you. Please, join us."* At that moment, one of the students, eyes still closed and hands raised, palms up, began to sing the most eloquent Native American song I'd ever heard. (Later, she explained that she had no knowledge of Native American songs, or of why she had begun to sing at that moment.) No one opened their eyes or moved during this entire event, except for the student who had gone looking for her keys. She came back and whispered to me that she couldn't figure out why her car's horn had gone off like that. Her car wasn't equipped with an alarm! Asking her to return to her seat, I completed the attunement, profoundly aware that I would forevermore request the assistance of my Native American healers at all times in the future when offering or teaching Reiki or participating in any form of peace prayer or ceremony.

Since that day, I have always honored that pledge. On almost every trip throughout the Sierra with my school's teachers, family, and/or friends, we have conducted prayer ceremonies requesting healing for humanity, especially for the Native Americans who have suffered atrocities since the "white man" landed in Jamestown, Virginia in 1607. (My direct ancestor, William Cox, arrived at Jamestown on the ship, Godspeed, in 1610.) It was during one of those Sierra trips that I experienced my second encounter with Chief Joseph. It happened in Lake Tahoe in June of 2006. (As I wrote this chapter, I realized that it had been exactly three years, *to the day*, since this event occurred.)

On the drive to Lake Tahoe, my school's program developer and massage instructor, Sandi Wolfe, and I underwent a very unusual series of healing exercises, sending young "warriors" via distance Reiki to war-torn areas of the world to bring "neutrality" to the soldiers in battle, since the world's leaders were not just yet responding fully to the *messages of peace from Spirit* that would be essential to the uplifting of humanity's frequency by the year 2012. My son, Steven, had just been deployed for a second tour of duty in Iraq. Because of this, my prayers were very intense. As we approached Lake Tahoe, Sandi and I joked that our ceremonies were now bordering on "whacko" status with this new assignment and that we may have to check ourselves into a mental ward when we got back home!

During the drive, Sandi mentioned that she really wanted to spend one afternoon of our three-day visit having lunch or dinner on a paddleboat cruise. I reminded her that our budgets were tight and that the paddleboat cruises were not cheap.

"I don't care," she said, "We're going!"

When we arrived at our hotel/casino, the car behind us in the valet area pulled a tad close as I stepped to the rear of my vehicle to open the trunk. "Watch out!" Sandi warned, thinking I might stumble backward into the path of the car. Actually, the driver had stopped several feet away.

The driver jumped out of her car and exclaimed, "Are you alright?"

"Sweetie, you didn't come near me." I shook my head, "I'm fine."

"Hold on a second." The driver walked around to her convertible's passenger side and opened a briefcase. Pulling out a card, she signed it and handed it to me, saying, "I'm the director of public relations for this hotel. I'd like to send you and your friend on a complimentary paddleboat cruise, including lunch." Thus began a very interesting Tahoe visit!

Entering the hotel/casino, we were upgraded to one of the V.I.P. suites with a balcony overlooking the lake. This was on a complimentary stay! The next day, we took the paddleboat lunch cruise. It was perfect. Without attracting attention (except from a few little Indigo children, who stared at us and waved discreetly when their parents weren't looking,) we resumed our "warrior-deploying" prayer ceremony while cruising around the lake. At one point, Sandi had a vision of an eagle with its wings spread wide.

Returning to the hotel/casino, we decided to attend the in-house theater that evening. It was now 4:30 in the afternoon. Sandi went off to play the slots for a while. Normally, I would have joined her in the casino. Instead, however, I felt intuitively that I needed to go upstairs to our suite. I wasn't tired. There was absolutely no reason for me to travel all the way across the casino, through the hotel registration area to the elevators and up to the sixth floor to our suite, which was at the far end of a long hall. I had injured my leg a month before in a fall and walking for any distance was difficult and painful. Sandi had even driven my car to Tahoe the day before because I was unable to drive. Now I was determined to walk, for no apparent reason, all the way to our suite!

Reaching the room, I stood silently, wondering what I should do next. Normally, I would have been downstairs playing a penny machine, trying to win my fortune. Ah, well. I decided to pour myself a glass of chardonnay and sit on the balcony for a while. Sitting in a chair, I propped my leg up on a small table and sipped the wine, watching the hotel's guests swimming in the pool below. I have always loved Lake Tahoe and it felt wonderful to be sitting there, relaxing and admiring the beautiful day. There were a few white, billowy clouds in the sky. The mountains around the lake were magnificent, as usual. I could have sat there all day and night.

While looking out upon this majestic scene, I was suddenly startled to see a huge beam of brilliant white light appear next to me on the balcony, only a few feet away. The beam of light was at least ten feet tall and two or three feet wide. I stared right at it, stunned. It lasted for a full two seconds, maybe three, then vanished. I was frozen in my chair, flabbergasted. Before I could even begin to try to comprehend what I had just seen, my attention was drawn to another startling sight.

Above the lake, slightly toward the left, there suddenly appeared a giant, perfect, white lightning bolt. It was enormous. Shaken, I began to

count—one/one-thousand, two/one-thousand, three/one thousand—
to determine in seconds how far away the lightning bolt was in miles.
I counted to ten seconds—about ten miles—midway across the lake.
Then *it* began—the rolling thunder. As the thunder clapped loudly
and began to roll toward me, it *spoke* to me in a deep, masculine voice,
saying, "*Do not disbelieve that your work is real. It matters. We value you.
We honor you.*" With this, the thunder rolled right up to and through
me. I was rooted in the chair. Before I could catch my breath, another
brilliant white lightning bolt appeared above the very center of the lake,
in exactly the same huge size and perfect shape as the first. Again, I
counted out ten seconds. As the thunder roared and rolled toward me,
it spoke again, "*Believe in your work. It is real. This is Joseph.*"

This time, as the thunder rolled toward me I was able to ask in reply,
"*How will I tell the others?*"

A third magnificent lightning bolt, identical to the first two,
appeared above the right third of the lake. Counting to ten, I again
heard the thunder's crackling roar as it began to roll toward me, saying:
"*Read the second line under my name below my statue . . .*" (Here he showed
me a vision of the property where his statue stands.) "*This is Joseph.*" I
knew which statue he was referring to. It was a ten-foot sculpture of
Chief Joseph that stood at the entrance to the Cal Neva Resort on the
north side of the lake. I had noticed it on a brief visit there years before;
however, I hadn't read the inscription on the monument and knew
nothing about Joseph then.

Still reeling from the experience, I was now firmly rooted in my chair.
The lightning and thunder were gone, yet I knew I still wouldn't be able
to stand up for a while. Minutes later, the door to our suite opened and
Sandi walked in. "Did you see that?" I yelled from the balcony.

"See what?" she asked, eyebrows raised, as she crossed the room.

"The lightning and thunder! It was huge!"

"No. I didn't hear any thunder."

"How could you miss it? You were sitting right next to the windows!
It was all over the entire lake!" I couldn't believe that anyone could have
missed what I had just witnessed.

"I didn't see or hear anything." she spoke softly, surprised at my intensity.

"Never mind. That's OK. Can we drive out to Cal Neva tomorrow?"

"Oh no, sweetie. I'm tired from the long drive yesterday and I don't really feel like driving all the way to the other side of the lake. Couldn't we just stay around here?" She did look tired.

"Yeah, that's OK," I relented. "We can stay here. I don't really need to go over there."

I knew that it wouldn't be necessary for me to prove to others what had just happened. Whatever was written on the monument's second line could only validate what I already knew beyond a shadow of a doubt. Joseph had spoken to me through his voice—*the thunder.* I would never forget what he had said. My work, my prayers for humanity to heal and awaken from the dream of illusion would continue for as long as I drew breath.

The next morning, I woke up to find Sandi standing, arms folded, at the foot of my bed. She was dressed and ready to hit the road. "Hurry up!" she said urgently, "Get dressed! We're going to Cal Neva!" Joseph must have visited her in the night! Throwing on my clothes, I rushed to the car with her. No coffee. No breakfast. Make-up on in the car. We're going to Cal Neva! It took almost an hour to get there because of ongoing roadwork on the highways. On the way, I told her about my experience on the balcony. She smiled, not speaking, the entire time.

When we finally arrived at the Cal Neva Resort, we approached the ten-foot statue of Chief Joseph that stands at the entrance to the property, marveling at its beauty. Suddenly, Sandi shrieked, "There it is!" She was looking up at the spread-winged eagle that she had seen during her vision on the paddleboat cruise. It was the top totem on a huge totem pole across the driveway from Joseph's statue.

I snapped her picture in front of the pole. Then, Sandi took my photo in front of the statue of Joseph. Famished, we started for the entrance to the resort, heading for the dining room and breakfast. As we began to climb the steps, I remembered what Joseph had said about the second line under his name. Turning back, I ran to the statue and read the inscription. The first line read, "Chief Joseph, chief of the Nez Perce` Tribe. Name—(IN-MUT-TOO-YAH-LAT-LAT.)" The second line, translating his name, read, "Thunder coming up over the land from the water." I cried all morning.

Since that day, Joseph has appeared to me and even to some of my friends several times, usually during a Reiki class or meditation. In my case, he first reappeared to me on a subsequent Lake Tahoe trip in the early night, awakening me from a deep sleep. Looking into my eyes, he thumped his chest with his closed fist and then, opening his palm, circled his face with his hand, ending by pointing his fingers toward me. I felt that he was saying to me, "I see you."

A few years later, I returned to Lake Tahoe with my daughter, Laura, and her mother-in-law, Carol, for the Fourth of July celebration. The fireworks were fantastic! And yes, Joseph visited me on the first night. I could see him with stark clarity. He said nothing, just looked into my eyes. (I think he might have been a little surprised I was writing this book!) On our third day in Tahoe, Laura and I visited his statue. It was sculpted by David Manuel in 1998. The inscription reads, *"We live, we die, and like the grass and trees renew ourselves from the soft clods of the grave. Stones crumble and decay. Faiths grow old and they are forgotten but new beliefs are born. The faith of the village is dust now, but it will grow again, like the trees. May serenity circle on silent wings and catch the whisper of the wind."*

*Chief Joseph*

During the next few years, I learned much more about Joseph and the Nez Perce`. They lived for centuries in their beloved Wallowa Valley in Oregon's northeast. When the Lewis and Clark expedition passed through Oregon, the Nez Perce` served as hosts and helped to guide them through the very steep terrain surrounding their valley and down the giant Columbia River. Joseph's father, Old Joseph died shortly after land disputes between the government and the Nez Perce` began. He was buried in his beloved valley. To young Joseph, it was unthinkable to leave the land of his father's grave. Many times before his death, Old Joseph had instructed his son to never allow his people to be taken from their home. Young Joseph served as Chief during the Nez Perce` war, when an unsigned treaty was forced upon him and his people, demanding that they be placed on an Indian reservation in another region of the state, bringing a peaceful society to a horrific conflict that lasted 89 days and covered over 1600 miles.

On the last day, only 40 miles from the Canadian border and safe refuge with his friend, Sitting Bull, Joseph surrendered to the frontier military, declaring, "From where the sun now stands, I will fight no more forever!" Many of his people had died on the treacherous journey. Some, including his wife and infant daughter, had escaped into Canada. His brother Ollokot, leader of the Nez Perce` warriors, was killed during the night. Joseph stayed behind with those who were unable to travel to the border in the freezing October night—the children and the elders. He was 37 years old. Even though his wife and daughter returned to Oregon years later, where they were placed on a reservation, Joseph was never allowed to see them again. He spent the remainder of his life on the Colville Indian Reservation in northeast Washington, where he died of a broken heart at the age of 64. During his incarceration, Joseph sat with three U.S. presidents and never stopped campaigning for his people to be returned to their beloved homeland and the resting place of his father, the Great Chief, Old Joseph.

Many books have been written about Joseph. My favorite is Candy Moulton's "Chief Joseph, Guardian of the People," a SPUR Award winner from the "American Heros" series. The movie, "I Will Fight No More Forever," produced by Heritage Entertainment, Inc., starring Sam Elliot, James Whitmore, and Ned Romero, provides a powerful reenactment of Joseph's story. Please watch it and join me in asking for healing for all participants. I'm sure that some of the frontier soldiers involved in the Nez Perce` war were descendants from my own ancestor, William Cox, so my prayers reach across both sides of the battle. Forgiveness heals.

In October of 2011, my daughter, Laura, and I visited the Wallowa Valley town of Joseph, Oregon. Named for Chief Joseph, the town is nestled in the remote valley and perched at the edge of the beautiful Wallowa Lake and Mountain Range. We spent four days visiting with the local residents and touring the sights. Now a destination resort town of 997, Joseph has become famous for its micro-beer-breweries and pubs. There is plenty of lodging in town and at the lake. Souvenior shops abound. There is even an 8,000 foot lift to a restaurant on the top of Mt. Stewart, named for the General who was Joseph's pursuer and, strangely, also his life-long friend. Laura and I rode the lift for 13 minutes to the top of the mountain and spent the afternoon sipping wine and feeding the squirrels. It was amazing to be sitting on a mountaintop looking across the lake's campgrounds to Mt. Joseph. I could feel the presence of the two great adversaries/friends as I reflected on their roles in our history.

That night, I awakened to a reception in my cabin. It was an OBE with full consciousness. In spirit, townspeople greeted us and traipsed through the building for hours. Finally, I slept. In the morning, I awakened to find Joseph as a young Indian boy peering at me from beside my bed. Instantly, he traveled through his lifetime in appearance, showing me his face as he aged. He was a very handsome young man, I noticed. The instant reveal stopped when he reached the age at which he usually appears to me, about fifty. For the first time, Joseph smiled. He looked so happy! And proud! I had never seen him smile before, neither in any of his appearances to me nor in any photo of him. (There are many.) I think he was very pleased and quite surprised that I was actually visiting his homeland. It had been a long drive to the Wallowa Valley from the Portland airport—about seven hours. We crossed several mountain ranges before we finally arrived at his beloved valley. Interestingly, my GPS failed and yet I knew exactly where to go! Of course, Joseph was guiding me. I felt that somehow my visiting his valley enabled him to also visit his valley—a sort of third dimensional event that needed to occur in real-time. While there, I visited the grave and monument of his father, Old Joseph. This was something that Joseph had never been allowed to do, since Old Joseph's grave-site had been dessicrated and subsequently moved to its current location atop the hill above Lake Wallowa. Joseph's only visit to his father's grave had been to its original site. He died a short time later.

On our last day in Joseph, we visited Lake Wallowa for a prayer ceremony. While there, I met two local young women. One of them, Melinda, had previously been attuned to 1st degree Reiki. They joined me in the prayer ceremony at the water's edge, where I also attuned them both to the next level of Reiki. One of the young women was an actual direct decendant of a Nez Perce` family that had escaped the Nez Perce` war and still lived in the Wallowa Valley a century and a half later!

After returning home, I received another visit from Joseph. It was during the night while I slept deeply. Suddenly, a brilliant light appeared over my bed and awakened me. Jesus was there in all of His glory and splendor, and Joseph was beside Him! Each was virtually encapsulated within a vast beam of brilliant light streaming from above. Jesus spoke to me in His exquisitely beautiful voice and, at the same time, His words were written out in front of me in white letters. I heard and read His message but was not able to recall it later. I'm sure, however, that it is sealed within my heart. I was trembling and crying and repeating, *"I love You,"* to Him while He was speaking to me, so I'm not surprised I can't remember what He said! Next, Joseph spoke in his eloquent tone. I will never forget what he said to me, as I'm sure it was meant for me to remember these words and repeat them here for you. They were stark in their simplicity and profound in their meaning. Joseph said, *"It is OK to have brown eyes or to have blue eyes. But if the eyes are brown, they should not also be worn and old looking."*

Joseph and the Nez Perce` never participated in judgement or predjudice. His people, his heritage, his message was always about honor and peace. He welcomed the white settlers to his valley and shared with them whatever he could offer. When he and his people were displaced, chased, killed, and imprisoned, he never lost his ability to forgive. I believe this is his message to us. On my nightstand is a picture of Joseph in full feather headress and this statement:

> *"Treat all men alike. Give them all the same law. Give them all the same chance to live and grow. All men were made by the Great Spirit*

*Chief. They are all brothers. The earth is the mother of all people, and all people should have equal rights upon it."*

Chief Joseph
Nez Perce`

I am deeply honored to have shared even one moment of my life learning about and visiting in spirit with Chief Joseph.

# AN ATTITUDE OF GRATITUDE

The one area that most reveals our path along the road to a more spiritual life is our attitude. If we are to restore our spiritual selves, embrace the shift in consciousness, and awaken from our collective dream, we need to uplift our *perspective* to a slightly different view—through *perception*, the lens of spirit, granting ourselves the gift of gratitude. Perspective gathers our five senses and arrives at a logical conclusion. With logical perspective, we can see that our glass is half empty and therefore lacking. When an attitude of gratitude is folded into the mix, our glass becomes half full and our perspective becomes a perception of fullness—allowing us to perceive our lives as more perfect, whole and complete. With this new perception, we can actually look around us and feel grateful for the people and conditions in our lives. Our hearts open to possibility. We no longer need to find ourselves in situations representing lack and limitation in order to appreciate what we have. We appreciate *everything*.

When you're feeling that your glass is half empty, resentment, sadness, depression, anger, guilt and blame become your common companions. These feelings are born of ego, and are actually part of the illusion created outside of Reality. In Truth, you are perfect, whole and complete. You have played a role, within the dream, that has given you an opportunity to experience the ramifications of perceiving yourself as less than perfect, whole and complete. When you shift your frequency up to the level of gratitude, which vibrates at a much higher rate that resentment, guilt and blame, you begin to appreciate your body, your family, your friends, your life and, most importantly, your Creator. As this happens, you begin to truly understand the power of forgiveness and compassion and you agree, in your highest moment, to give up the one thing you no longer need in your life—your fear of experiencing yourself as perfect, whole and complete. When this happens, you may find yourself looking away from your dream for just a moment to discover that your are, always have been, and always will be *Home with God*.

*Welcome Home* . . . .

# THE HEALING SANCTUARY

In 2005, I read just-released books from two of my favorite authors. The first was "Prophesy" by Sylvia Brown. Sylvia is one of America's foremost psychics, appearing regularly on the Montell Williams talk show and "reading" his quests. She has written many books on the spiritual side of life and I've enjoyed reading them through the years. "Prophesy", particularly, captured my attention because it described events from the future, an area of special interest for me. I had experienced "time-travel" in some of my OBEs in the past and was delighted to see that Sylvia had witnessed some of the same future events that I had encountered. One of Sylvia's prophesies involved holistic health and wellness centers. In her vision, she saw "wellness centers" springing up in neighborhoods across America. These wellness centers offered holistic health modalities that included a variety of massage therapies, Reiki, aromatherapy, herbs, etc. from trained therapists. These are among the very same modalities that are taught at my school, the Holistic Life Institute.

The second book that caught my attention that summer was "Secrets of the Light", by Dannion Brinkley. Dannion detailed a spiritual experience in which he, also, was shown a future with "wellness centers" in every neighborhood in America that offered many of the same healing modalities! While reading this book, I found myself suddenly at the base of a beautiful waterfall thundering in front of me. I was boating on Lake Pinecrest in the Sierra Mountains with my sister and her husband when the waterfall appeared in the middle of the lake! We all witnessed it. Just before it appeared, I had prayed for a sign that would indicate that my school would be a part of the training for the practitioners who would eventually staff the envisioned "wellness centers". To this day, I cannot find the beautiful waterfall on Lake Pinecrest. It seemed to appear out of nowhere that day! I believe that it was my confirmation. Since then, HLI has been training teachers who will someday train the staff for those many wellness centers. In the meantime, a beautiful property in the sierra foothills only twenty minutes from our campus has become available to us. I plan to build a holistic retreat for weekend guests in search of spa treatments, a holistic hospital for guests in need of more extensive healing, and an intensive campus for students who are either traveling from a distance or who need to complete their training in less time. Go to our web-site at www.holisticlifeinstitute.com for updates if you are interested in attending any of these facilities. Also, find us on facebook as Jan Noble, Oakdale or Holistic Life Institute, Oakdale. I post classes, events and openings on both pages.

# FREQUENCY ELEVATORS

In this chapter, I will outline the 20 steps to elevating your frequency that, coupled with the meditations and exercises in the book, should enable you to visit *Home*. Please send me your stories. The next *Home With God* book will be filled with stories provided by my readers. Also, you may want to attend one of our Kaua'i trips to participate in our global peace prayers. Please contact me through my school's website for details and dates at www.holisticlifeinstitute.com.

## 1) Light therapy:

If you suffer from S.A.D. (seasonal affective disorder), you may not be getting enough sunlight on the back of your eyelids or enough Vitamin D on your skin. Both of these steps are essential to elevating your frequency. Fifteen minutes of direct sunlight (before 11:00 a.m. or after 3:00 p.m. to avoid dangerous rays) will provide the ideal amount. If you live in an area of low sunlight or winter-time darkness, you can use an indoor light-bulb. Close your eyes and face the bulb for up to three minutes. Don't get too close. You are close enough when you can feel the warmth of the bulb on your nose. Within a few minutes, your frequency will increase, giving you more energy and vitality. Also, a Vitamin D supplement will help compensate for the lack of sunlight.

## 2) Bodywork:

I recommend five types of bodywork to elevate your frequency. You can pick and choose or try all five, depending on your preference. Each of these modalities will release endorphins to facilitate healing and raise your frequency—Reiki, Swedish massage, Cranial-Sacral Balancing, EFT (Emotional Freedom Technique) and Acupuncture. You can find qualified therapists on-line for your area. Be sure to ask for their credentials, certificates and/or licenses. Consider taking a Reiki class. If you would like to study Reiki at my school, e-mail me for dates of my next seven-day Reiki intensive in Kaua'i or on campus. We're located next-door to a Holiday Inn. E-mail Jan@Holisticlifeinstitute.com.

## 3) Hydrotherapy:

Alternating hot (or very warm) water with cold (or very cool) water is a very powerful method for releasing endorphins to relieve pain and stiffness. Pain lowers our frequency. Natural pain relief facilitates increased frequency. In the shower, use the warmest temperature that is comfortable for two minutes, followed by the coolest temperature that is comfortable for about one minute. Repeat three times, ending on cool. Wrap in a large towel or sheet around yourself and lie down, remaining still, for 30 minutes. Do this daily for two or three weeks and you will discover a whole new world of healing!

## 4) Stopping smoking, drugs and alcohol:

Sorry, these three habits are absolute deal-breakers. It is almost impossible to elevate your frequency if you smoke and use drugs or alcohol to excess. Of course, prescription drugs are fine, if they are prescribed for you only. Substance abuse, however, will always decrease, not increase, frequency. A glass of wine or an occasional cocktail shouldn't lower your frequency too much, as long as it's not a daily thing.

## 5) Restoration prayer:

Repeat this prayer as often as possible. It raises frequency like nobody's business.

"Divine Creator, Father/Mother/Son as One:

"With every breath, I breathe in Your healing light through the center of my heart, allowing Your light to expand, encompassing all of my bodies, known and unknown, on all levels, past, present and future, on all dimensions, time-frames and locations, forward and backward and retroactive, abolishing ego and restoring Spirit. Let this be written in the Book of Life, so let it be done this ____ day of _____ , in the year _____ . (birth name) _____ , (birth date) _____/_____/_____.

"Thank You, God."

## 6) Prosperity/Health/Etc. Prayer:

Repeat this prayer, also, as often as needed. It really works! Fill in the blanks as you wish.

"I now call forth the quality of _____ (Prosperity/Health/Love/Peace/etc.). I can feel the energy of the quality of _____ coming to me, coming out from someplace inside of me, filling me up, and radiating out from me. I give thanks and gratitude for this quality of _____ now, and so it is. Let this be written in the Book of Life. "Thank You, God."

## 7) Yoga and/or Tai Chi:

For thousands of years, practitioners of yoga and Tai Chi have known about the spiritual benefits of both of these graceful modalities. Try them both out until you find the one you resonate with. Videos abound. Watch your frequency soar!

## 8) Aromatherapy:

Essential oils have one of the highest frequencies of all known substances on earth. Contact Young Living Essential Oils (www.YLEO.com). Or, just visit your local health food store. There are many excellent brands. Place the oils on your feet morning and night. Inhale. Diffuse into your home. Flood your life with oils! (Contact Debbie Libhart, CMT, Aromatherapy Instructor, through our web-site—www. holisticlifeinstitute.com.)

## 9) Flower Essences:

Another amazing natural frequency elevator. Flower Essences, like essential oils, carry some of the highest frequencies on earth. They also release emotional baggage that can keep our frequency low. Go to www.perelandra-ltd.com or www.pegasusproducts.com or look for Bach Flower Remedies at your local health food outlet. For a crash course in high-frequency healing, order the book, *Flower Essences and Vibrational Medicine*, by Gurudas.

## 10) Blue/Green algae or Spirulina:

This is one of our earth's most abundant foods and offers the highest frequency from nutrition. Go to www.IVLProducts.com (All Day Energy Greens) or www.puritan.com (Puritan's Pride) to order. You can also find a "green formula" in most health food stores.

## 11) Alkalizing your acidic body:

Excess acid ph in your body lowers your frequency and sets the stage for disease. Go to www.phion.com to order alkalizing supplements. Order the Acid/Alkaline Diet book from them to find out how to get healthy and stay healthy. Your frequency will vibrate up!

## 12) Meditation:

This one essential frequency elevator cannot be underestimated. Meditation is the single most effective way, next to prayer, to raise your frequency and access the higher spiritual planes. It is said that when we pray, we talk to God, and when we meditate, God talks to us. I have first-hand experience that this is true. Go to www.onespirit.com for a wide selection of meditation CDs, if you need assistance. (Just doing the meditation exercises in this book should be enough, but variety is, after all, the spice of life!)

## 13) Reading A Course in Miracles:

Order the course from www.amazon.com if you want to buy a used copy for about half-price. I did, and mine is a collector's item. The cover is on upside down! Go to www.acourseinmiracles.com or www.facim. org for information. *A Course in Miracles* was actually "dictated" by Christ in the late 1960s and early 1970s. You will recognize His voice and presence when you read from the text. The information in the course is the most important message, I believe, of our time, and the most direct route *Home*.

## 14) See God in everyone:

This may take some practice, but it is so worth it in the long run. As you converse with others, remind them silently that they are the Child of God and that there is only one of us here. Watch their demeanor change before your very eyes! "Namaste'" says "When you are one with spirit and I am one with spirit, we are one with each other." Try it.

## 15) Dedication Prayer:

In your own words, dedicate to your divine purpose through Christ. For a book of dedication prayers, go to www.livinglightcenter.com.

## 16) Ceremony:

"Wheresoever two or three are gathered in my name," miracles happen. Wedding ceremonies, prayer ceremonies, church ceremonies, graduation ceremonies, reunion ceremonies, get the picture? Celebrate life! High frequency loves ceremonies. (Nix the booze.)

## 17) The Beauty Way; Vitamin C, body wraps, MSM (sulfur):

A diet deficient in Vitamin C will lower your frequency faster than anything. Your body is held together by Vitamin C (collagen). Avoid disease; take 1500 mg to 2000 mg of Vitamin C per day. Plant some fruit trees, preferably citrus. Go to www.credence.org. Join the Campaign for Truth in medicine. Body wraps help to detoxify your cellular structure from low-frequency toxins. MSM (sulfur) is formulated in our foods after rain waters the crops. Sulfur's precursor, DMSO, is formed in the clouds. (Sulfur is what makes snow white.) If you live in an area that is suffering from drought, you may be deficient in sulfur (not to be mistaken for sulfa, to which many people are allergic). If you have fibromyalgia pain or stiffness, you may be deficient is sulfur. Again, pain lowers your frequency. Apply sulfur gel to the areas of your body that hurt. It's completely natural and cannot be overused. Apply several times for the maximum benefit. Go to www.msmclearsolution.net to order.

## 18) Strengthen your immune system:

Take a vitamin supplement that combines a proprietary blend of nutrients for optimum results. Go to www.puritan.com for excellent prices. Drink lots of water filtered with charcoal, if necessary. Bottled water contains chemicals in the plastic that can easily leach into the water from heat and light. Go to www.water-disaster.com to find out why. Drink the cocktail described in this book (based on chai tea.) This drink virtually rebuilt my mom's immune system. Use Himalayan Pink salt in your bath and as a tonic to alkalize and strengthen your immune system. Look up *"**Sole made from Himalayan Salt Benefits**"* online and follow the easy recipe to make your own tonic. You will be amazed at the results. I began to notice marked improvements in energy levels within days!

## 19) Join or start a prayer group:

A regular get-together with like-minded friends and family is essential to keep us on track. Go to www.spiritualcinemacircle.com to get started. Tell James that I sent you. I told him about this book, and that he was mentioned in it, the last time I saw him. He was presenting at the "Celebrate Your Life" expo in Scottsdale, Arizona. He'll be happy to hear from you.

## 20) Surrender it all:

When you're ready, and I hope that you are, tell God that you surrender your life, your work, your children, your body, your mind, your family, your friends, your very existence, totally and completely to Him. He'll take it from there. Trust me. Namaste!

# CONCLUSION

I sincerely hope you've enjoyed my stories. Please read them often if you did. Every time I reread this book, my frequency increases. The words bring me closer to *Home with God* every time I re-read them, even though I wrote them. I'm hoping this will be true for you, too.

# RECOMMENDED READING

Braden, Gregg, *Awakening to Zero Point: The Collective Initiation*. Sacred Spaces Ancient Wisdom, 1995.

_____, *Mystery of 2012: Predictions, Prophecies and Possibilities*. Carlsbad, CA: Hay House, 2007. ISBN-13: 9781401909970

_____, *Speaking the Lost Language of God*. Carlsbad, CA: Hay House, 2005. ISBN-13: 9781401909970

_____, *The God Code*. Carlsbad, CA: Hay House, 2005. ISBN-13: 9781401903008

Melchizedek, Drunvalo, The Ancient Secret of the Flower of Life (vol. 1&2). Flagstaff, AZ: Light Technology Publications, 1999.

_____, *Through the Eyes of a Child* [VHS]. Lightworks Audio & Video, 2000. ASIN: B000053V33

*Drunvalo Melchizedek*
*Go to www.earthskyheart@aol.com*
*Or www.drunvalo.net*

Arguelles, Jose, *Earth Ascending: An Illustrated Treatise on the Law of Whole Systems*. Shambhala Publications, Inc., 1984. ISBN-13: 9780877732631

_____, *The Mayan Factor: Path Beyond Technology*. Bear & Company, 1987. ISBN-13: 978-0939680382

*EFT (Emotional Freedom Technique) by Gary Craig*
*Go to www.emofree.com*

*"Indigo, The Movie" and "The Indigo Evolution"*
*By James Twyman, Neale Donald Walsch and Stephen Simon*
*www.spiritualcinemacircle.com*

*"The Surf Report" by Solara at www.nvisible.com*
*Also by Solara,*
*"11:11" (the universal code for the shift of 2012)*

*"Quantum Healing" by Deepak Chopra, MD*
*Go to www.thechopracenterforwellness.com*

*Dr. Rath, vitamin C researcher, www.drrathresearch.com*

*All of the other authors referenced in this work are listed, with their book's titles, in the text. For more information and additional references, go to www. holisticlifeinstitute.com.*

# The Thief in the Night

A golden glow shimmers in the night
I feel a sense of something very right
A quickening electrifies my heart
Suddenly I'm waking with a start

He bundles me gently in His arms
I know beyond a doubt there is no harm
Like a trusting child I go without a fight
Abducted by the Thief in the Night

He cloaks me in His robes and we soar
Through the night to the inner door
Past the stars shining in the sky
As softly He begins to tell me why

Once upon a time I fell asleep
Asking that my soul He would keep
Innocent of fear that I might
Be abducted by the Thief in the Night

Now my window glows in candlelight
A beacon for the Thief in the Night

CPSIA information can be obtained
at www.ICGtesting.com
Printed in the USA
FSOW01n1551100315
5643FS

9 781452 548050